TELEVISION FAST FORWARD

TELEVISION FAST FORWARD

Sequels & Remakes of Cancelled Series
1955-1992

Updated & Revised Edition
LEE GOLDBERG

Text copyright © 2015 Adventures in Television
All rights reserved.
No part of this book may be reproduced, or stored in a retrieval system, or transmitted in any form or by any means, electronic, mechanical, photocopying, recording, or otherwise, without express written permission of the publisher.

Adventures in Television
PO Box 8212
Calabasas, CA 91372

ISBN: 1511590769
ISBN-13: 9781511590761

To Valerie, for everything

PREFACE TO THE 2015 EDITION

This book was originally published in 1992 and was a labor of love for me. It was a book I wanted to read and, since nobody else had written it, I wrote it myself out of frustration.

There have been dozens of television series revivals since then…enough for another book, which I hope to write some day, because I am still a big TV geek. In the mean time, I've only updated series that were in the first edition that have been revived yet *again* since then. All of the other TV revivals and remakes produced since 1992 are listed in two appendices at the end of the book.

In addition to adding that new stuff, I've also deleted the entries on the new *Twilight Zone*, *Alfred Hitchcock* and *Ultraman* that were in the previous edition because they do not meet the inclusion criteria for the book. So why were those shows included in the first edition? My ego got in the way of my good sense. I'd written articles about those three shows, interviewed the key creative talent involved, and even visited the sets of the new *Twilight Zone* and *Alfred Hitchcock* during production. I thought I had some really good stuff and I wanted to save it for posterity. So I came up with a lame justification for shoe-horning the material into the book. That was a mistake. I'm older and wiser now or maybe my ego has simply deflated a bit, though I think that's unlikely.

I hope you enjoy this new edition!

Lee Goldberg
May 23, 2015

vii

ACKNOWLEDGMENTS

The information in this book is culled from the shows themselves, network press releases, reviews, and magazine and newspaper articles. All of the people quoted in this book were interviewed by me unless otherwise noted.

I am indebted to my various editors over the years—Dave McDonnell, Janet Huck, Jerrold Footlick, Ron Givens, David Klein, Ron Aldridge, Richard Mahler, Morrie Gelman, Michael Carmack and Julie Benson—for giving me the opportunity to cover television revivals in depth for *Starlog, Newsweek, Electronic Media* and the Los Angeles Times Syndicate. This book could not have been done without their generous support.

In addition, I would like to thank George Faber at Viacom and John Wentworth and Larry McCallister at Paramount for supplying much-needed information, and William Rabkin for supplying much-needed patience. Also, a very special thanks to Burl Barer, with whom I co-wrote the "Maverick" listing.

Whenever possible, the information in this book was cross-referenced against previously published material. A complete list of those books can be found in the bibliography.

CONTENTS

INCLUSION CRITERIA

This book includes new versions of television series that featured continuing characters. To be included in this book, the shows must truly be "revivals," not simply series moving to a new broadcast outlet (e.g. from network to first-run syndication) or evolving into a new format after a short hiatus. A series has to have been canceled, and out of production, for two years for a new movie, pilot, or series to be considered a revival.

Revivals are listed by the original series' title, followed by the network which aired them and the years they were broadcast. Each listing includes an overview of the characters and how they've changed between the original show and the revival, a plot synopsis, and, in some cases, details behind the making of the program. Finally, each listing concludes with production information on each revival, sequel, or remake.

There is an appendix listing details about the animated revivals of prime-time, live-action shows, such as "Star Trek" and "Gilligan's Island." Animated versions of live-action shows that aired while the primetime shows were still being broadcast ("Emergency: Plus Five," "The Brady Kids," etc.) are not included. And there are two appendices of TV revivals & remakes produced from 1992 to mid-2015.

The following categories of shows are not included:

Shows based on literary characters. For example, series about the Saint, Robin Hood, and Sherlock Holmes aren't really continuations or sequels, but simply new versions of old literary properties, and hence do not qualify as television revivals (unless the new versions are *direct* continuations of the television story, rather than the books, and feature the original actors. An example of this would be "Perry Mason").

Anthologies, variety shows, and game shows, as they have no continuing characters.

Shows from other countries, with the exception of "The Avengers," which aired in primetime in the United States.

Finally, "The Honeymooners" is not included because it is a very special case and because it would take a book of its own to catalog all the programs (and there have been several) featuring the Kramdens and the Nortons. "The Honeymooners" began as a variety show skit, later became a beloved sitcom, and then continued for decades as skits in variety shows and specials. More a continuing enterprise than a series, "The Honeymooners" does not really qualify as a show that was canceled and then revived.

INTRODUCTION TO THE 1992 EDITION

They are like old friends,

    We grew up with them.

    Perhaps we outgrew them, or they outgrew us. Or one day we went to look for them, and they were gone. And like all old friends we haven't seen in a while, we might wonder what they're doing today. After all, we remember them as they were, the time we spent with them in our living rooms each week.

    Is Marcus Welby still making house calls? Did Gilligan and his friends ever get rescued? Did Dr. David Banner ever tame the raging beast that dwelt within him? What kind of father did Beaver Cleaver turn out to be? Is Marcia Brady, the girl we all had a crush on, still single and available? What happened after the starship *Enterprise* ended its five-year mission?

    They were more than just characters to us, they were almost real. It's no wonder, then, that we have gone back and visited so many of them. Throughout the 1980s and into the 1990s, television has embraced its past with a passion bordering on obsession. Even the motion picture, music, and publishing industries got caught up in the frenzy.

    On television, there was Matt Dillon taming the West again. In the theaters, Capt. Kirk duked it out with aliens while Lt. Frank Drebin was slipping on banana peels. In record stores, one had a choice of Mr. Ed or Mister Mister. And in bookstores, the life and times of Oliver North shared the shelf with "The Life and Times of Maxwell Smart."

    It was not simply nostalgia that made the television industry so compulsively, and exhaustively, revisit its past. There are three variables that sparked the revival business: dwindling network viewership, the high mortality rate of new series, and the emergence among independent television stations of a concept called "barter syndication."

Before the 1980s, the three commercial networks simply fought among themselves for the viewing audience. The battlefield was prime time television, the soldiers were new series, and the body count was tabulated by Nielsen ratings.

It was a comfortable existence.

Then everything changed, thanks to cable and VCRs. In the 1980s, the networks found themselves running scared, looking over their shoulders at newcomers like the Fox and USA networks, HBO, MTV, the Disney Channel, CNN, home video, and the coalitions of independent stations which are now producing their own network-quality series.

The good old days were gone. The question facing ABC, CBS, and NBC was how to get them back. The sage advice has always been that you can't live in the past–but nobody said you can't recreate it. So the networks heightened their well-honed practice of feeding on themselves. When they were warring among each other, they would spin off new shows from venerable hits (e.g., "All in the Family" begat "The Jeffersons") to attract audiences. Exhuming old series, then, was a new variation on an old theme, and it began in 1978, when NBC's "Rescue from Gilligan's Island" copped a whopping 52 share of the audience and Paramount's *Star Trek: The Motion Picture* earned $100 million worldwide.

Turning reruns into first-runs was a revelation, a way to turn lead into gold. Suddenly any series that had been off the air for a decade was a hot commodity. There were more and more revivals airing more and more frequently. The practice reached insane proportions when "Maverick" was brought back three times in three years, once on each network. But that was only the beginning.

Revivals became so pervasive that by the late 1980s, the network schedules looked like a page torn out of a yellowed *TV Guide*. Switch on the set, and who did we see, all dressed up like new? Perry Mason, Columbo, Kojak, the Incredible Hulk, even Alfred Hitchcock. The networks were asking viewers to relive the glory days of television and rekindle their fondness for it. The nostalgia ploy was designed to hold the viewers the networks still had and reclaim some of those who had strayed to other media. Cable, not to be outwitted, was willing to feed on old television, too. Showtime revived "The Paper Chase," USA exhumed Alfred Hitchcock, and the Disney Channel, for a time, produced "Still the Beaver." Even the motion picture industry, which had used movie remakes and sequels in a similar ploy for years, began scavenging in the television scrap heap, pulling out big-screen versions of "Star Trek," "Get Smart," "The Twilight Zone," and "Police Squad."

Meanwhile, the networks were becoming less tolerant of shows that failed to perform up to expectations. Out of the six or seven shows a network might introduce in the fall, it was miraculous if one survived to see its first birthday. This trigger-happy attitude left a dearth of programming available as reruns for syndication–and, in effect, the networks inadvertently created a monster that became strong competition and, ironically, a new source of television revivals.

The mainstay of independent station programming is reruns. Stations are looking for series with enough episodes to permit one to be run each weekday for a year or more. Within the industry, this practice is called "stripping." The value of a show "off-network" is a combination of its popularity and the number of episodes it has available to strip.

Ideally, stations look for well-known series that have 80–100 episodes, the equivalent of roughly a three- to four-season run on network television. Shows with 60–70 episodes, like "Matt Houston" and "Vega$," are often useful for summertime, when stations "rest" their popular reruns for a few months.

The dwindling number of off-network sitcoms with enough episodes to strip did not keep pace with the heavy demand for reruns. And those that *were* available were outrageously expensive. In fact, the price tag on off-network series tripled between 1980 and 1985. So television stations, tired of being gouged, and producers, infuriated by premature cancellation and the lost opportunity to accumulate episodes for off-network syndication, fought back.

When NBC's Emmy award-winning "Fame" was canceled in 1983, MGM put it into first-run syndication and offered it to stations on a "barter" basis. What does that mean? Simply put, a first-run syndicated show is too expensive for stations to buy, so it is given to them essentially for free. In return, the stations give the distributor several minutes of commercial time to sell to national advertisers. This is called barter syndication. There are variations. In cash-plus-barter, shows are sold to stations for a fee plus advertising time. Another method involves a complicated formula in which stations share in the potential "back end," or rerun revenue from stripping, down the line. "Fame" became a huge hit, a syndication breakthrough that was quickly followed by "Too Close for Comfort" and a slew of revivals of short-lived series like "It's a Living," "9 to 5," and "What's Happening!" While original first-run series had a hard time finding buyers, stations embraced the retreads with unrestrained enthusiasm.

The allure of reviving an old series as opposed to developing an original program was simple. The networks were the ones footing the cost of development, and with a revival they could hand to stations a program for which they did not have to build an audience from scratch.

Using barter syndication, independent stations mastered the art of mining revivals for every last audience share and advertising dollar. First-run syndication became glutted with revivals of series nobody watched in the first place. So why did they come back? Dollars.

In network television, the quality of a show gets it on the air, but in first-run syndication it is the quality of the deal. Artistic merit is a low priority. Selling reruns, and making back deficits incurred during the network runs, is the goal. Why else would anyone even think of something as absurd as "That's My Mama Now"?

The glut of first-run, deal-based sitcom revivals got to the point that Gary Lieberthal, chairman and chief executive officer of Embassy Communications, once joked: "I wonder if sometime in the future, halfway through a season, TV stations will put a crawl in front of the opening credits: 'Dear viewer—please excuse the quality of this show, but it was a great deal.'"

That day, of course, didn't come, but there was the inevitable shake-out. While deal-based revivals continued (à la "Baywatch"), the barter syndication market was also supporting revivals based on genuine merit *and* a great deal—like "Star Trek: The Next Generation" and "Super-boy."

It may not be just the tough, competitive nature of prime time, or the new strategies of barter syndication, that has provoked television to look back. "You could make a whole case about America going back to isolationism, patriotism," says Greg Maday, a former CBS executive now developing shows for Warner Bros. Television. "Within the last few years you could say we've gone back to those shows that reflected those values."

"It doesn't take a genius to figure it out," says Anthony Masucci, formerly NBC's vice president of made-for-television movies. "In the sixties we had lots of kids watching television who are now our age. They are the most desirable viewers now and these are the shows they loved." But can one really say that about "Cannon" or "Crazy Like a Fox"?

Perhaps, too, revivals represent the natural growth of a medium reaching middle age. "Had television started fifteen or twenty years earlier than it did, you would have seen revivals in the early sixties," says Lloyd Weintraub, a development executive for Viacom, the production company behind "Perry Mason Returns." "It has nothing to do with bad shows today or the success of other revivals. Fifteen years from now people will want to know what happened to the characters in 'Hill Street Blues' or 'Miami Vice' perhaps." The movie studios are already mounting, or considering, such diverse fare as "The Fugitive" (with Harrison Ford as Dr. Richard Kimble and Tommy Lee Jones as Inspector Gerard), "Hawaii 5-0," "Beverly Hillbillies," "The Brady Bunch," "Hill Street Blues," and even "F-Troop."

"As long as the public demonstrates an interest, as long as we can find a reason to do them, we will do them," says Masucci. "There is a finite number, but that depends on how far back you want to reach."

At a certain point we may very well catch up with ourselves. But that probably will not stop anybody. Watch out. Can "Three's Still Company" and "Spenser: Still for Hire" be far away?

But there's more to television revivals than network panic, studio greed, and shrewd marketing. When television revivals work, when the affection for the characters is genuine, they undeniably strike an emotional chord and have a resonance beyond simply good business.

We have grown up with television. There is something comforting about seeing those familiar faces again, even if the hair is gray, the paunches more pronounced, and the smiles not as sparkling. For that hour or two, we are not just anonymous television viewers sitting alone in our living rooms—we are plugging into a big, cultural, family reunion, sharing fond memories and old friends. And despite the crass manipulation of it all, that's still pretty special.

TELEVISION FAST FORWARD

Adam-12
NBC (9/21/68–8/26/75)

Officers Jim Reed (Kent McCord) and Pete Malloy (Martin Milner) are gone, but their squad car remains, now driven by officers Gus Grant (Peter Parros) and Matt Doyle (Peter Wayne).

Background

The only new variation in the revival was that one of the officers, Peter Parros, was black. Otherwise, it was more of the same, only not as good as the original.

The series was a companion piece to "The New Dragnet," which shared the same creative staff.

"The New Adam-12"

Syndicated. 44 episodes (1990). Production Company: Universal Television, Arthur Company. Executive Producers: Arthur Annecharico, Burton Armus, Craig Kellem. Producer: John Whitman. Creators: Jack Webb, R.A. Cinader; developed by Burton Armus. Story Editors: Joseph Gunn, E. Nick Alexander.

Cast. Officer Gus Grant: Peter Parros. Officer Matt Doyle: Peter Wayne. Sgt. Harry Santos: Miguel Fernandes.

The Addams Family
ABC (9/18/64–9/2/66)

The Addamses are exactly as we left them ten years ago. When Gomez goes out of town to a convention, he's nervous about leaving his family in the care of his brother Pancho (Henry Darrow), who is as attracted to Morticia as he is. Little does he know there are more important things to worry about–like criminals who, disguised as Morticia and Gomez, are plotting to steal the Addams fortune while the family is hosting a Halloween party.

Background

"The Addams Family Halloween" was a tedious, lackluster affair that was an embarrassment even to producer David Levy, who had worked on the original series. He told Stephen Cox in the book "The Addams Family Chronicles" that he had little control over the project, which he characterized as "a good example of network, bureaucratic interference depriving audiences of the values that were inherent in the project."

He eventually proved his point when, over a decade later, a 1991 theatrical version of Charles Addams' comic strip characters (with a plot similar to the television reunion), featuring the unmistakable, finger-snapping Vic Mizzy television theme, was a box office sensation for Paramount Pictures.

"Addams Family Halloween"

NBC TV movie, 90 minutes (10/30/77). Production Company: Chuck Fries Productions. Director: Dennis Steinmetz. Executive Producer: Charles Fries. Producer: David Levy. Writer: George Tibbies. Creator: David Levy. Music: Vic Mizzy.

Cast. Gomez Addams: John Astin. Morticia Addams: Carolyn Jones. Wednesday Addams: Lisa Loring. Pugsley Addams: Ken Weatherwax. Lurch: Ted Cassidy. Grandmama: Jane Rose. Ophelia Frump: Carolyn Jones. Esther Frump: Elvia Allmann. Cousin Itt: Felix Silla. Pancho Addams: Henry Darrow. Wednesday Addams, Jr.: Jennifer Surprenant. Pugsley Addams, Jr.: Kenneth Marquis.

See also "The Addams Family" in the Appendix.

A.E.S. Hudson Street
ABC (3/25/78–4/20/78)

The adventures of chief resident Dr. Tony Menzies (Gregory Sierra) and his belea-guered staff at New York's Hudson Memorial Hospital, Adult Emergency Service.

Among his co-workers were administrator J. Powell Karbo (Stefan Gierasch), pregnant nurse Rosa Santiago (Rosana Soto), paramedic Foshko (Susan Peretz), ambulance driver Stanke (Ralph Manza), gay nurse Newton (Ray Steward) and interns Dr. Jerry Mackler (Bill Cort) and Dr. Gloria Manners (Barrie Youngfellow).

Over a decade later, Menzies (now Dennis Boutsikaris) is still at work, and has a new team around him. There's intern Dr. Elizabeth Newberry (Alison La Placa), Dr. Lewis Doniger (Casey Biggs), Nurse Anderson Roche (Ron Canada), and orderly Julio Oscar (Julio Oscar Mechoso).

Background

Danny Arnold's sitcom about a hospital lasted for half a dozen episodes—and 12 years later, when he remade it as "Stat," it fared no better. F. Murray Abraham played Menzies in the 1977 pilot, Gregory Sierra stepped in for the short-lived series, and Dennis Boutsikaris came in for the flop remake. Boutsikaris and his co-star Alison La Placa would later reteam on "The Jackie Thomas Show." The original series was created by Danny Arnold, Tony Sheehan, and Chris Hayward.

"Stat"

ABC. Six episodes (4/16/91–5/21/91). Production Company: Tetragram Ltd. Touchstone Television. Executive Producer: Danny Arnold. Producers: Chris Hayward, John Bunzel. Story Editor: Samuel Shem. Music: Jack Elliott.

Cast. Dr. Tony Menzies: Dennis Boutsikaris. Dr. Elizabeth Newberry: Alison La Placa. Dr. Lewis Donigar: Casey Biggs. Jeanette Lemp: Alix Elias. Andy Roche: Ron Canada. Julio Oscar: Julio Oscar Mechoso. Dr. Ron Murphy: Wren T. Brown.

Jim Nabors, George Lindsay, Don Knotts, Andy Griffith
and Ron Howard in "Return to Mayberry."

The Andy Griffith Show
CBS (10/3/60–9/16/68)

Andy Taylor (Andy Griffith) and his wife Helen (Aneta Corsaut) moved
to Cleveland in 1968, where Andy worked as a postal inspector. He
returns to Mayberry–where his son Opie (Ron Howard) is newspaper

editor and, with wife Eunice (Karlene Crockett), an expectant father–to run for sheriff, only to learn that his former deputy, Acting Sheriff Barney Fife (Don Knotts), still engaged to Thelma Lou (Betty Lynn) after 25 years, is also vying for the post, which he has been temporarily holding since the last sheriff passed away. Gomer (Jim Nabors), long back from his stint in the Marines, owns a garage with Goober (George Lindsay), and Otis (Hal Smith), once the town drunk, has sobered up and now sells ice cream. While the election is hot news in town, what really has folks gossiping is a mysterious monster in the lake–which turns out to be a publicity stunt by a sleazy businessman to bring tourists to Mayberry and customers to his restaurant. Before long, Opie becomes a daddy, Barney marries Thelma Lou, and Andy is elected sheriff, promptly hiring Barney as his deputy once again.

Background

Lots of folks had talked about doing a revival, but Andy Griffith shrugged it off until he, Don Knotts, and Ron Howard got together as presenters at an Emmy Awards show.

"Ron came up to me and said, 'Are you going to the big party afterwards?'" recalled Griffith. "I said, 'Don and I are going to dinner.' I saw the look on his face and said, 'Would you like to come along?' He sure did. We must have sat there for three or four hours just talking about old times, and that's how we got the idea."

Just about everyone returned for the revival, which effectively captured the flavor and gentle humor of the original series, something few reunion shows can pull off. The only actors missing were Howard McNear, who played Floyd the Barber (he died in 1967), and Frances Bavier, who was too ill at the time to resume her role as Aunt Bee.

"All these people are kind of the same people they always were," Griffith said. "Mayberry is a little town in North Carolina that still exists with the same values it had 25 years ago."

It was a revival behind the camera as well. Director Bob Sweeney helmed 100 of the original series' 249 episodes, writers Harvey Bullock and Everett Greenbaum penned 60 of the originals, and composer Earle Hagen whistled the original theme.

"Return to Mayberry"

NBC TV movie, two hours (4/13/86). Production Company: Viacom Productions. Director: Bob Sweeney. Executive Producers: Andy Griffith, Dean Hargrove, Richard O. Linke. Producer: Robin S. Clark. Writers: Harvey Bullock, Everett Greenbaum. Music: Earle Hagen.

Cast. Sheriff Andy Taylor: Andy Griffith. Opie Taylor: Ron Howard. Deputy Barney Fife: Don Knotts. Gomer Pyle: Jim Nabors. Goober Pyle: George Lindsay. Otis Campbell: Hal Smith. Howard Sprague: Jack Dodson. Thelma Lou: Betty Lynn. Ernest T. Bass: Howard Morris. Briscoe Darling: Denver Pyle. Butler: Richard Lineback. Charlene Darling: Maggie Petersen. Eunice Taylor: Karlene Crockett. The Darlings: Rodney Dillard, Doug Dillard, Dean Webb, Mitch Jayne.

The Avengers
ABC (3/28/66–9/15/69)

When we last saw John Steed (Patrick MacNee), he and agent Tara King (Linda Thorson) were headed into outer space on an errant rocket. Well, Steed has returned to Earth and has teamed up with two young agents, ex-ballerina and martial arts expert Purdy (Joanna Lumley) and Mike Gambit (Gareth Hunt), a former **SAS** officer and ex-mercenary. While the younger agents do most of the dirty work, Steed relaxes on his country farm, breeding horses and occasionally seeking spy-chasing advice from Mrs. Peel (Diana Rigg), reunited with her long-lost husband and retired from espionage, double-entendres, and leather jumpsuits.

Background
An inferior follow-up to the enormously popular original series brought the Avengers back in an international coproduction that fell prey to financial troubles and was canceled after just two seasons. Patrick MacNee conceded the show was "awful" in a 1991 interview with Karl Shook for *Starlog* magazine.

"I think 'The New Avengers' was perfectly awful, and the main reason it was perfectly awful was because I was in it," he said. "They didn't offer it to Diana Rigg or Linda Thorson, and they shouldn't have offered it to me. What they should have done was say, 'We are going to make "The Avengers" with two young people.' Why the hell they put me in it, I don't know. Why I accepted it, I don't know. They lost any sense of 'The Avengers,' and the whole thing, to me, was a mishmash."

"The New Avengers" eventually ran late nights on CBS, which liked the show enough to order an American version set in San Francisco from a most unlikely source: producer Quinn Martin, famed for such turgid cop shows as "Barnaby Jones" and "The FBI." Martin, however, had the good sense to hire "Avengers" creator/producer Brian Clemens to write the one-hour pilot, entitled "Escapade," which starred Granville Van Dusen and Morgan Fairchild, aired once on May 19, 1978 and disappeared into oblivion immediately thereafter.

A theatrical version of "The Avengers," starring Ralph Fiennes and Uma Thurman as Steed and Peel was released in 1998 and was a critical and financial bomb.

"The New Avengers"

CBS. 60 minutes, 26 episodes (9/15/78–3/23/79). Production Company: Avengers Enterprises Ltd., IDTV TV Productions Paris, Neilsen-Ferns Toronto. Producers: Brian Clemens, Albert Fennell. Associate Producer: Ron Fry. Music: Laurie Johnson.

Cast. John Steed: Patrick MacNee. Purdey: Joanna Lumley. Mike Gambit: Gareth Hunt.

"Escapade"

CBS. 60 min. Airdate: 5/19/78. Production Company: Quinn Martin Productions. Director: Jerry London. Executive Producer: Quinn Martin. Producer: Philip Saltzman. Writer: Brian Clemens. Creator: Brian Clemens. Music: Patrick Williams.

Cast: Joshua Rand: Granville Van Dusen, Susie: Morgan Fairchild. Arnold Tulliver: Len Birman. Paula: Janice Lynde. Wences: Alex Heteloff Seaman: Gregory Walcott, Charlie Webster: Dennis Rucker.

Vince Edwards in "Return of Ben Casey."

Ben Casey
ABC (10/2/61–3/21/66)

When we last saw Dr. Ben Casey (Vince Edwards), he was resident neuro-surgeon at County General Hospital, working closely with his mentor, Dr.

David Zorba (Sam Jaffe), chief of neurosurgery. Since then, he has served as a combat surgeon in Vietnam, spent five years with the aborigines in Australia, and worked for 12 years as chief of surgical service at Milwaukee County. Now, he returns to County General as new acting chief of neurosurgery, and is attempting to put his life back together, to regain his sense of purpose and, someday, renew ties with his estranged son Patrick (from a failed marriage to a woman named Kate), who won't even come to talk with him on the phone. Along the way, he locks horns with the icy hospital administrator (Gwynyth Walsh), and becomes mentor to a new group of young doctors, much like Zorba was to him.

Background

This attempt at launching a new, first-run "Ben Casey" syndicated series was shot in Canada and seemed dated coming on the heels of shows like "St. Elsewhere" and "Medical Story."

"Return of Ben Casey"

Syndicated TV movie, two hours (1988). Production Company: Columbia Pictures Television. Director: Joseph Scanlan. Executive Producer: Robert Cooper. Producer: Julian Marks. Writer: Barry Oringer. Creator: James E. Moser.

Cast. Ben Casey: Vince Edwards. Dr. Stratton: Al Waxman. Dr. Ted Hoffman: Harry Landers. Rita Gillette: Gwynyth Walsh. Dr. Jacobs: Jason Blickner. Street Kid: Lynda Mason Green. Dr. Madigan: August Schellenberg. Kyle: Torquill Campbell. Blaine: Joanne Vannicola. Dr. Burnside: Tracy Moore. Dr. Dowling: Allan Katz. Dr. Brown: Teddi Lee Dillon. Dr. Samadji: Dale Azzard. Dr. Hollis: Cassandra Edwards. Bernard: John Stocker. Randall: Gary Reineke. Wigham: Jerry Haig. Gates: Linda Smith. Nurse Lowell: Barbara Harris. Hill: Griffin Brewer. Kelly: Chantall Condor. Resident: Declan Hill.

Buddy Ebsen and Donna Douglas in *The Beverly Hillbillies* in 1960s and in 1981.

The Beverly Hillbillies
CBS (9/26/62–9/7/71)

The Clampetts, the hillbilly family that struck oil in the Ozarks and moved to Beverly Hills, are still the same at heart a decade later. Jed Clampett (Buddy

Ebsen) has moved back to the Ozarks, Elly Mae (Donna Douglas) has opened a zoo, and Jethro now runs a movie studio. Jane Hathaway is now an energy department official who realizes that Granny's potent moonshine is the perfect solution to the nation's energy crisis.

Or...not. In 1993, they surviving members of the family gathered together to reminisce for a documentary. The filmmakers found Jed living in the Ozarks, swindled out of his fortune by his banker, Milburn Drysdale, who was now in prison. Drysdale's assistant, Miss Hathaway, who'd testified against him, was in the witness protection program. Jethro had become a Beverly Hills doctor and Elly Mae was still taking care of animals.

Background

For the first revival, Ray Young stepped in as the new Jethro, and Imogene Coca guest starred as Granny's 100-year-old mother. The second revival in 1993 was a "mocumentary" that treated the Clampetts as if they were real people and featured cameos by celebrities (and the fictional Douglases from "Green Acres") who'd known the hillbillies. The special, essentially a clip show, aired the same year that a feature film remake of the series was released. Buddy Ebsen appeared in the movie, not as Jed Clampett, but as another one of his TV characters, private eye Barnaby Jones.

"The Beverly Hillbillies Solve the Energy Crisis"

CBS TV movie, two hours (10/6/81). Production Company: CBS Productions. Director: Robert Leeds. Executive Producers: Albert J. Simon, Ron Beckman. Producer: Paul Henning. Writer: Paul Henning. Music: Billy May.

Cast. Jed Clampett: Buddy Ebsen. Ellie Mae: Donna Douglas. Jane Hathaway: Nancy Kulp. Jethro Bodine: Ray Young. Great Granny: Imogene Coca. CD Medford: Werner Klemperer. Linda: Linda Henning. Andy Miller: King Donovan. Mollie Heller: Lurene Tuttle. Chief: Charles Lane. Judge Gillim: Shug Fisher. Veterinarian: Howard Culver. Also: Heather Locklear, Shad Heller, Earl Scruggs, Nancy Gayle, Dana Kimmell, Fenton Jones, John Hartford, Rodney Dillard, Buddy Van Horn.

"The Legend of the Beverly Hillbillies"

CBS Documentary/Clip Show. 60 minutes. (5/24/93) Production Company: CBS Productions, Imaginary Entertainment. Director: Jay Levey.

Cast: Jed Clampett: Buddy Ebsen. Jethro Clampett: Max Baer Jr. Oliver Wendall Douglas: Eddie Albert. Lisa Douglas: Eva Gabor. Ellie Mae Clampett: Donna Douglas. Sonny Drysdake: Louis Nye. Also, Hoyt Axton, Mac Davis, Ray Charles, G. Gordon Liddy and Reba McEntire, as themselves.

The Bionic Woman
(See Six Million Dollar Man)

The Bob Newhart Show
cbs (9/16/72–9/2/78)

Psychologist Bob Hartley (Bob Newhart), with his wife Emily (Suzanne Pleshette), never did move to Oregon to accept a teaching position at a small college. Instead, he stayed in Chicago, where he has turned to his friends Jerry Robinson (Peter Bonerz), Howard Borden (Bill Daily), Carol Kester Bondurant (Marcia Wallace) and his patient, Mr. Carlin (Jack Riley), to help him come to grips with a disturbing dream–that he was an innkeeper in Vermont–on the eve of the 19th anniversary of his practice.

Jerry is still a dentist, Howard is still an airline navigator, Carol is still Bob's receptionist/secretary, and Mr. Carlin remains Bob's patient, except for a brief period when he was in the psycho ward of Boston's St. Eligius hospital, aka St. Elsewhere, where he shared a room with a guy who thought he was Mary Richards, the character played by Mary Tyler Moore on her long-running sitcom.

Background

In 1990, CBS enjoyed extraordinary success with a weekend of retrospectives about "All in the Family," "The Mary Tyler Moore Show," and the "Ed Sullivan Show." In 1991, hoping to score again, they aired retrospecitves of "M*A*S*H," the "Ed Sullivan Show," and "The Bob Newhart Show." The

Bob Newhart special was unique, using the classic final episode of his subsequent, and perhaps more popular, series "Newhart" (which concluded with Bob Hartley waking up and realizing the events in "Newhart" were all a bad dream) as the springboard for a mini-revival, in which Hartley goes to his friends and patients to help him analyze his weird dream. Together, they remembered past events, and we got treated to vintage clips. Although it was the most inventive of the three specials that aired the weekend of November 23, 1991, Newhart's was the lowest-rated.

"Bob Newhart 19th Anniversary Special"

CBS Special. 60 minutes (11/23/91). Production Company: MTM Enterprises. Executive Producers: George Zaloom, Les Mayfield. Producer: Jean-Michel Michenaud. Writers: Michael Mahler, Mark Egan, Mark Soloman.

Cast. Bob Hartley: Bob Newhart. Emily Hartley: Suzanne Pleshette. Howard Borden: Bill Daily. Jerry Robinson: Peter Bonerz. Elliott Carlin: Jack Riley.

Bonanza
NBC (9/12/59–1/16/73)

The year is 1905, and time has left its mark on the Ponderosa, Ben Cartwright's massive ranch just outside Virginia City. Now that Ben has died, his seafaring brother Aaron (John Ireland) has come to run the ranch, with the help of seasoned foreman Charlie Pogue (Robert Fuller). Ben Cartwright saved Pogue's life, standing up to an angry mob and cutting the man down from a hanging. Ever since, Pogue has pledged his life to protecting the Cartwrights and the Ponderosa.

Pogue is taking a bit more than a protective interest in Annabelle Cartwright (Barbara Anderson), who hopes that her husband Little Joe, who disappeared years ago while serving with Teddy Roosevelt's Rough Riders at San Juan Hill, will one day return and help her raise Benji (Michael Landon, Jr.), their headstrong son who comes back from an East Coast school driving one of them newfangled automobiles.

They are joined by strapping giant Josh (Brian A. Smith), an illegitimate child who comes to the Ponderosa looking to kill his father, Hoss. Josh learns that Hoss drowned rescuing a woman in a river–which is why Hoss never returned to marry Josh's mother (and, of course, why Hoss never got around to mentioning her name to the Cartwrights).

The whole family finds itself facing a crisis when the Ponderosa is imperiled by money-grubbing Cal Dunson (Peter Mark Richman), who tricks Aaron into letting him do some exploratory mining–and putting the increasing numbers of unemployed folks in Virginia City to work. In fact, Dunson rapes the land with illegal hydraulic mining and, once revealed, has no intention of giving up his search for gold, regardless of what the Cartwrights want.

But good, naturally, wins out over evil, and honest miners are put to work–as are twice as many unemployed citizens. And it looks like Aaron just might live up to the memory of Ben Cartwright.

Unfortunately, Aaron passes away soon after that and the responsibility of running the ranch for the Cartwrights is taken over by seasoned ranchhand Bronc Evans. Soon Bronc and the family find themselves battling a Augustus Brandenburg, a land baron intent on acquiring the Ponderosa by any means necessary in order to strip mine its natural resources. Joining in the fight to save the Ponderosa is Adam's long-lost son, arriving in Nevada from distant Australia. In a trivia note of interest to fans, Annabelle tells Josh that she knew Hoss well; in fact, Hoss was best man at her wedding to Little Joe. Of course, when Hoss died in the original series, Little Joe was unwed. Little Joe did eventually get married, but his wife was murdered. The movie was shot entirely on location at Ponderosa Ranch, Incline Village, Nevada.

Background

Luck was not on David Dortort's side as he mounted a revival of his classic series for first-run syndication. Lorne Greene died shortly before production, forcing a rewrite and the casting of John Ireland as Ben's never before mentioned brother. The producers were also unable to reach an agreement with Dan Blocker, Jr. to play the son of Hoss, the character his father portrayed until his death. Although five scripts were ordered, plans for a new series were derailed by the six-month-long Writers Guild of America strike, which hit Hollywood shortly after the pilot aired.

Four years later, NBC showed interest in another revival. John Ireland had died…so Aaron Cartwright was out, replaced by Ben Johnson as ranch hand Bronc Evans, who ran the ranch and served as the Lorne Greene-esque father-figure. Michael Landon, Jr. was back as Little Joe's son, and Brian Leckner replaced Brian A. Smith as Josh, Hoss' son. One more sequel followed, but NBC lost interest.

In 2001, the fledgling PAX network launched "Ponderosa," a short-lived prequel series that was shot in Australia. It was produced by Beth Sullivan, creator of "Dr. Quinn: Medicine Woman."

"Bonanza: The Next Generation"

Syndicated TV movie. Two hours (March 1988). Production Company: Bonanza Ventures Ltd., Gaylord Productions, LBS Communications. Director: William Claxton. Executive Producers: William F. Claxton, Thomas W. Sarnoff, Alan Courtney. Producers: Stacy Williams, David Dortort. Writer: Paul Savage; story by David Dortort. Creator: David Dortort. Music: Bob Cobert. Theme: Jay Livingston, Ray Evans.

Cast. Aaron Cartwright: John Ireland. Annabelle Cartwright: Barbara Anderson. Charlie Pogue: Robert Fuller. Benji Cartwright: Michael Landon, Jr. Josh Cartwright: Brian A. Smith. Jennifer Sills: Gillian Greene. Mr. Mack: John Amos. Mr. Dunson: Peter Mark Richman. Nathaniel Amstead: Kevin Hagen. Gus Morton: William Benedict. Sheriff Montooth: Richard Bergman. Sills: Dabs Greer. Eldon Poole: Gary Reed. Mayor: Lee McLaughlin. Feathers: Robert Hoy. Cease: Rex Linn. Deke: Jerry Catlin. Lundeen: Jeffrey Meyer. Cullen: Robert Jaurequi. Homer: Jeffrey Boudou. Rachel: Laurie Rude. Mover-Shaker: Clayton Staggs.

"Bonanza: The Return"

NBC. Two hours (11/28/93). Production Company: Legend Entertainment, NBC Productions. Director: Jerry Jameson. Executive Producers: David Dortort, Thomas W. Sarnoff. Co-Executive producers: Tom Brinson, E.K.

Gaylord II. Producers: Kent McCray. Writer: Michael Landon. Jr., Michael McGreevey. Creator: David Dortort. Music: Bruce Miller. Theme: Jay Livingston, Ray Evans.

Cast. Bronc Evans: Ben Johnson. Annabelle Cartwright: Barbara Anderson. Charlie Pogue: Robert Fuller. Benji Cartwright: Michael Landon, Jr. Josh Cartwright: Brian Leckner. Adam Cartwright Jr.: Alistair McCougall. Jacob Briscoe: Richard Roundtree. Buckshot: Jack Elam. Augustus Brandenburg: Dean Stockwell.

"Bonanza: Under Attack"

NBC. Two hours (1/15/95). Production Company: Legend Entertainment, NBC Productions. Director: Mark Tinker. Executive Producers: David Dortort, Thomas W. Sarnoff. Co-Executive producers: Tom Brinson, E.K. Gaylord II. Producers: Kent McCray. Writer: Denne Bart Petitclerc. Creator: David Dortort. Music: Bruce Miller. Theme: Jay Livingston, Ray Evans.

Cast. Bronc Evans: Ben Johnson. Annabelle Cartwright: Barbara Anderson. Charlie Pogue: Robert Fuller. Benji Cartwright: Michael Landon, Jr. Josh Cartwright: Brian Leckner. Jacob Briscoe: Richard Roundtree. Charlie Siringo: Dennis Farina. Frank James: Leonard Nimoy. Cole: Ted Markland. Mears: Kenny Call. Adam Cartwright: Jeff Phillips. Buckshot: Jack Elam.

"Ponderosa"

PAX. Series. 60 minutes. 20 episodes. (September 9, 2001 – May 12, 2002) Executive Producer: Beth Sullivan, David Dortort. Producers: Tim Johnson, Glen Aveni.

Cast: Adam Cartwright: Matthew Carmody. Ben Cartwright: Daniel Hugh Kelly. Hoss Cartwright: Drew Powell. Little Joe: Jared Daperis. Frenchy: Brad Dourif. Margaret Green: Josephine Byrnes. Carlos de Vega: Fernando Carillo. Shelby Sterritt: Nicky Wendt. Hop Sing: Gareth Yuen

The Brady Bunch
ABC (9/26/69–8/30/74)

When we last saw the Bradys, they were still the irrepressibly upbeat clan of three boys and three girls, going through one wacky hijink and zany adventure after another. But three years later, in 1977, they move to a house on the beach and get their own variety show and star-studded bell-bottoms. Unexpected guests like Lee Majors, Tina Turner, Vincent Price, Redd Foxx, and Paul Williams drop by to sing and dance, but soon architect Mike Brady (Robert Reed) and his wife Carol (Florence Henderson), now a realtor, are back in the same old familiar house, preparing for the double wedding of clothing designer Marcia (Maureen McCormick) to toy designer Wally Logan (Jerry Houser) and architecture student Jan (Eve Plumb) to Phillip Covington III (Ron Kuhlman), a chemistry professor. Getting everyone together for the big event isn't easy–Alice (Ann B. Davis) married Sam the Butcher (Allan Melvin) and moved away, Peter (Christopher Knight) is in the Air Force, Bobby (Mike Lookinland) is in college, and Greg (Barry Williams) is a busy gynecologist. But everyone makes it, and the two sisters get married, in typically wacky Brady fashion.

Not only are Marcia and Jan getting married in one ceremony, but the couples plan to live together under one roof! Can life get any zanier? You bet. At one point, conflicts get so heated they have to divide the house in half by hanging a sheet down the middle!

It's no wonder the Brady brides eventually move apart, and in the next seven years, there are many other changes. Marcia and Wally and their two kids grin and bear Wally's unemployment; Jan and Phil are having marital problems; electronics salesman Peter is miffed because he makes less than his fiancée; Bobby is dropping out of grad school to race cars; and Greg and his wife Nora (Caryn Richman), a nurse, are so busy they hardly see each other.

Still, the burgeoning bunch get together for a family Christmas at their parents' house. And just when it seems like everyone's problems are solved, Mike has to rush off to investigate a problem at one of his construction sites–and gets trapped in a cave-in. Luckily, the site is on 34th Street, and Mike and his entire crew are "miraculously" unhurt.

But there are troubles ahead–Bobby gets in a race car accident and is wheelchair bound, perhaps for life. But he takes the setback courageously and with humor, and everyone is hopeful for his complete recovery, no one more than his devoted wife Tracy (Martha Quinn), his college sweetheart. Meanwhile, the bunch keeps getting bigger as new problems confront the upbeat Bradys. Jan and Phillip adopt an Asian girl, Greg and Nora have a son, and the Brady house is zoned for demolition to make room for a new freeway. But Mike Brady moves the house to a new location and decides to run for city council, letting Jan take over some of his responsibilities at the firm. Meanwhile, Cindy (Susan Olsen) becomes a hit DJ and falls for her handsome, widowed boss, becoming a step-mom to his daughter. And Marcia has a dangerous flirtation with alcohol, but no one in the Brady bunch is ever down for long. Everything turns out well, and the charmed lives of the Bradys, America's favorite family, seem destined to continue well into the future.

Background

"The Brady Bunch Variety Hour," coming three years after "The Brady Bunch" was canceled, was a ridiculous attempt at merging a revival with a variety show. While most of the cast returned, creator/ writer /producer Sherwood Schwartz and the rest of his creative team did not. The series was mounted by Sid and Marty Krofft, perhaps best known for such children's shows as "Sigmund and the Sea Monster," and "Donny and Marie." "The Brady Bunch Variety Hour" evolved from a guest-shot on the latter show by some of the Brady kids.

Following on the heels of Schwartz's success with "Rescue from Gilligan's Island," NBC commissioned a more traditional reunion of "The Brady Bunch." Programmers were so impressed with "The Brady Girls Get Married," it was decided to edit it into a two-part launch of a spin-off series, "The Brady Brides," which lasted six weeks in 1981.

But that didn't deter CBS from launching "A Very Brady Christmas," which was the runaway hit of 1988, scoring an amazing 25.1/39 and prompting the network to immediately order three more movies. However, while the Brady sequels were in production, the network was getting decimated on Friday nights. Desperate for ratings, CBS opted to cut the movies into one-hour episodes and launch a new series dubbed "The Bradys." They learned a hard lesson: baby boomers may rush home to watch a special reunion of a beloved show, but not every week. "The Bradys" fared no better than "The Brady Brides" and was quickly canceled.

Robert Reed and Florence Henderson in
"The Brady Bunch Variety Hour."

"The Brady Bunch Variety Hour"

ABC. 9 episodes (1/23/77–5/23/77). Executive Producers: Sid and Marty Krofft. Director: Jack Regas. Producer: Lee Miller. Co-Producer: Tom Swale. Music: George Wyle. Writers: Carl Kleinschmitt, Ron Graham, Bruce Vilanch, Steve Bluestein, Michael Kagan.

21

Cast. Mike Brady: Robert Reed. Carol Brady: Florence Henderson. Alice: Ann B. Davis. Marcia Brady: Maureen McCormick. Jan Brady: Geri Reischl. Cindy Brady: Susan Olsen. Greg Brady: Barry Williams. Peter Brady: Christopher Knight. Bobby Brady: Mike Lookinland.

"The Brady Brides" (aka "Brady Girls Get Married")

NBC. 9 episodes (2/6/81–4/17/81). Production Company: Paramount Television. Executive Producer: Sherwood Schwartz. Producers: Lloyd Schwartz, John Thomas Lenox. Music: Frank DeVol.

Cast. Mike Brady: Robert Reed. Carol Brady: Florence Henderson. Alice: Ann B. Davis. Marcia Brady: Maureen McCormick. Jan Brady: Eve Plumb. Cindy Brady: Susan Olsen. Greg Brady: Barry Williams. Peter Brady: Christopher Knight. Bobby Brady: Mike Lookinland. Phillip Covington: Ron Kuhlman. Wally Logan: Jerry Houser.

Ann B. Davis joins the family in the hit special "A Very Brady Christmas."

"A Very Brady Christmas"

CBS TV movie (12/18/88). Production Company: Paramount Television. Executive Producer: Sherwood Schwartz. Producer: Lloyd Schwartz. Director: Peter Baldwin. Writers: Sherwood & Lloyd Schwartz.

Cast. Mike Brady: Robert Reed. Carol Brady: Florence Henderson. Alice: Ann B. Davis. Marcia Brady: Maureen McCormick. Jan Brady: Eve Plumb. Cindy Brady: Jennifer Runyon. Greg Brady: Barry Williams. Peter Brady: Christopher Knight. Bobby Brady: Mike Lookinland. Phillip Covington: Ron Kuhlman. Wally Logan: Jerry Houser. Nora: Caryn Richman. Jessica: Jaclyn Bernstein. Mickey: J.W. Lee. Kevin: Zachary Bostrom. Valerie Thomas: Carol Huston.

Greg (Barry Williams) and his wife Nora (Caryn Richman)
watch Bobby crash on television in "The Bradys."

"The Bradys"

CBS. 6 episodes (2/9/90–3/9/90). Production Company: Paramount Television. Executive Producers: Sherwood Schwartz, Lloyd Schwartz. Producer: Barry Berg. Music: Laurence Juber.

Cast. Mike Brady: Robert Reed. Carol Brady: Florence Henderson. Alice: Ann B. Davis. Marcia Brady: Leah Ayres. Jan Brady: Eve Plumb. Cindy Brady: Susan Olsen. Greg Brady: Barry Williams. Peter Brady: Christopher Knight. Bobby Brady: Mike Lookinland. Phillip Covington: Ron Kuhlman. Wally Logan: Jerry Houser. Nora: Caryn Richman. Jessica: Jaclyn Bernstein. Mickey: Michael Malby. Kevin: Jonathan Weiss. Valerie Thomas: Carol Huston. Patty: Valerie lek. Tracy: Martha Quinn.

Cannon
CBS (9/14/71–9/19/76)

Frank Cannon (William Conrad) hasn't lost any weight, and running a restaurant of his own probably hasn't helped. Gone are the days of catching crooks; now he just catches fish for his cook (James Hong) to prepare. But that changes when an old friend from his days in the CIA is murdered. Cannon investigates and, along the way, rekindles an old flame with his dead friend's widow (Diana Muldaur). Once he solves the mystery, he accepts the fact he can't leave private detecting entirely behind.

Background

One of the more mind-boggling revivals—was anybody really interested in seeing "Cannon" again? Even if they were, the result wasn't so great. As *People* magazine noted, the plot of this pilot "lumbers along as heavily as its star."

"The Return of Frank Cannon"

CBS TV movie. Two hours (11/1/80). Production Company: Quinn Martin Productions. Director: Corey Allen. Executive Producer: Quinn Martin. Producer: Michael Rhodes. Writers: James David Buchanan, Ronald Austin. Music: Bruce Broughton. Theme: John Parker.

    Cast. Frank Cannon: William Conrad. Yutong: James Hong. Sally Bingham: Diana Muldaur. Alana Richardson: Joanna Pettet. Mike Danvers:

Ed Nelson. Charles Kirkland: Burr DeBenning. Curtis McDonald: Arthur Hill. Jessica Bingham: Allison Argo. Lew Garland: Taylor Lacher. William Barrett: William Smithers. Pearson: Hank Brandt.

Car 54, Where Are You?
NBC (9/17/61–9/8/63)

These are the misadventures of Officer Gunther Toody (Joe E. Ross) and his partner Officer Francis Muldoon (Fred Gwynne) as they haplessly patrol the Bronx in Car 54. They are close friends with many other officers on the force, including 20-year veteran Officer Leo Schnauzer (Al Lewis) and Officer Anderson (Nipsey Russell).

Background

A musical, feature film version of "Car 54, Where Are You?" was made by Orion Pictures in 1991, starring David Johansen (aka singer Buster Poindexter) as Officer Muldoon and featuring Al Lewis returning to his role as Schnauzer, who now spends most of his time watch "The Munsters" (Lewis played "Grandpa" on that show). However, the film got caught up in the messy bankruptcy of Orion Pictures (the same studio that made *The Addams Family* feature and then had to sell it to Paramount for some quick cash) and, by the time it was eventually released in 1994, all the music numbers had been cut.

"Car 54, Where Are You?"

Theatrical (produced in 1990, released 1994) 90 minutes. Production Company: Orion Pictures. Director: Bill Fishman. Producers: John M. Eckert, Robert H. Solo. Writer: Eric Tarloff, Ebbe Roe Smith, Peter McCarthy, Peter Crabbe. Music: Dan Wool, Bernie Worrell

    Cast: Officer Gunther Toody: David Johansen. Officer Francis Muldoon: John C. McGinley. Velma Velour: Fran Drescher. Capt. Dave Anderson: Nipsey Russell. Lucille Toody: Rosie O'Donnell. Don Motti: Daniel Baldwin.

Herbert Hortz: Jeremy Piven. Leo Schnauzer: Al Lewis. Mrs Muldoon: Barbara Hamilton. Also, Penn Jilette as himself.

Charles in Charge
CBS (10/30/84–7/24/85)

Charles (Scott Baio) is a college student who becomes a live-in babysitter of sorts for Jill and Stan Pembroke (Julie Cobb, James Widdoes) and their three children. He still finds time to study, chase girls, and hang out with his dimwitted friend Buddy (Willie Aames). But when Charles goes off on a two-week vacation, he returns to discover the Pembrokes gone, and their house leased to the Powells–Ellen (Sandra Kerns) and her kids, high schooler and model-in-training Jaime (Nicole Eggert), teenage wannabe writer Sarah (Josie Davis), and ten-year-old Adam (Alexander Polinsky). With her husband Robert (James O'Sullivan) spending long months at sea as a naval commander, Ellen relies on Charles and her father-in-law Walter (James Callahan), a retired Navy officer himself, to help her raise the family. Charles' mother Lillian (Ellen Travolta) now runs the local pizza parlor where he and Buddy like to hang out.

"Charles in Charge"

Syndicated. 30 minutes (1987–1990). Production Company: Universal Television. Executive Producer: Michael Jacobs. Producers: Al Burton, Jane Starz.

   Cast. Charles: Scott Baio. Buddy Lembeck: Willie Aames. Ellen Powell: Sandra Kerns. Jaime Powell: Nicole Eggert. Sarah Powell: Josie Davis. Adam Powell: Alexander Polinsky. Walter Powell: James Callahan. Lillian: Ellen Travolta.

Peter Falk in the original "Columbo" series.

Columbo
NBC (9/15/71–9/1/78)

Columbo still drives the same car. Still wears the same rumpled overcoat. Still smokes the same cigars. And still drives clever, arrogant murderers crazy with his endless stream of seemingly innocuous questions.

Background

"Columbo" returned, and it was as if he never left. Peter Falk won an Emmy for his portrayal of Columbo, beloved not just in America but abroad as well.

In 1989 ABC attempted to use "Columbo" as the linchpin of its "ABC Mystery Movie," through none of the other elements–"Christine Cromwell," "Gideon Oliver," "Kojak," or "B.L. Stryker"–measured up.

27

Instead, "Columbo" went on to become a series of television movies in its own right, following the example set by the "Perry Mason" movies. By January 1992, there were enough segments that ABC began airing "Columbo" reruns on a weekly basis.

In March 1992, ABC radically altered the now-classic Columbo formula in "No Time to Die," based on an Ed McBain novel, and opted instead to try what could easily have been a leftover "Kojak" plot. When the bride of Columbo's nephew is kidnapped on her wedding night, the famed detective tracks her down. Although critics and diehard fans deplored the dramatic departure, audiences tuned in anyway, making it one of the network's highest rated movies of the season.

"Columbo"

ABC TV movies. Two hours (1989-2003). Production Company: Universal Television. Executive Producers: William Link, Peter Falk, Jon Epstein. Producers: Christopher Seiter, Todd London. Creators: Richard Levinson, William Link. Story Editor: William Reed Woodfield. *Cast:* Lt. Columbo: Peter Falk.

The Movies:
"Columbo Goes to the Guillotine" (2/6/89)
"Murder, Smoke and Shadows" (2/27/89)
"Sex & the Married Detective" (4/3/89)
"Grand Deceptions" (5/1/89)
"Murder: A Self Portrait" (11/25/89)
"Columbo Goes to College" (12/9/90)
"Columbo Cries Wolf" (1/20/90)
"Agenda for Murder" (2/10/90)
"Rest in Peace, Mrs. Columbo" (3/31/90)
"Columbo: Uneasy Lies the Crown" (4/28/90)
"Columbo: Murder in Malibu" (5/14/90)
"Caution: Murder Can Be Hazardous to Your Health" (2/20/91)
"Columbo and The Murder of a Rock Star" (4/29/91)
"Death Hits the Jackpot" (10/15/91)
"No Time to Die" (3/15/92)
"A Bird in the Hand" (11/22/92)
"It's All in the Game" (10/31/93)

"Butterfly in Shades of Grey" (1/10/94)
"Columbo Undercover" (5/2/94)
"Strange Bedfellows" (5/8/95)
"A Trace of Murder" (5/15/97)
"Ashes to Ashes" (10/8/98)
"Murder with Too Many Notes" (3/12/2001)
"Columbo Likes The Nightlife" (1/30/2003)

Crazy Like a Fox
CBS (12/30/84–9/4/86)

The Fox family–P.I. Harry Fox (Jack Warden), his uptight lawyer son Harrison (John Rubinstein), his daughter-in-law Cindy (Penny Peyser) and grandson Josh (Robbie Kiger), are vacationing in London when Harry is accused of murdering a duke and must prove his innocence.

Background

Although the show left the air in September 1986, its death warrant was signed in April, when it was murdered by "Dynasty" in the weekly ratings, barely mustering a meager 19 share. Herman Rush, then president of Columbia Pictures Television, wouldn't accept it. "The show still has legs. They never gave us a chance. We deserve to be back on the air."

The pilot, which the studio referred to as "simply episode #36," was shot entirely in England. The studio planned to offer the revival into first-run syndication if CBS turned it down. Apparently, the fickle independent stations, which also rejected Columbia's "The Return of Ben Casey" and "That's My Mama Now!," weren't interested.

"Still Crazy Like a Fox"

CBS TV movie. Two hours (4/5/87). Production Company: Shulman/Baskin/Schenck/Cardea Productions, Columbia Pictures Television. Director: Paul Krasny. Executive Producers: George Schenck, Frank Cardea. Producer: Bill Hill. Writers: George Schenck, Frank Cardea.

Cast. Harry Fox: Jack Warden. Harrison Fox: John Rubinstein. Cindy Fox: Penny Peyser. Josh Fox: Robbie Kiger. Nancy Church: Catherine Oxenberg. Inspector Palmer: Graham Chapman. Randall Perry: Michael Jayston. William Church: James Faulkner. Mrs. Eleanor Trundle: Rosemary Leach.

Dark Shadows
ABC (6/27/66–4/2/71)

The Collins family seems destined to relive its past. Their story unfolds once more when Victoria Winters comes to Collinsport, Maine, and imposing Collinwood estate, to tutor troubled nine-year-old David. There she becomes embroiled in the twisted, supernatural past of the Collins family, and becomes the obsession of vampire Barnabas Collins, who believes she is the reincarnation of his long-dead lover.

Background

The new "Dark Shadows" was essentially a big budget rerun, a primetime remake of the daytime gothic/horror soap, right down to the scripts, which were condensed rewrites of the decades-old originals (storylines which took weeks or months in the original soap spanned only an episode or two in the remake). The revamped vampire serial lasted only 13 weeks.

"Dark Shadows"

NBC. 60 minutes, 13 episodes (1/13/91–3/22/91). Production Company: MGM/UA Television. Executive Producer: Dan Curtis. Producers: Steve Feke, Jon Boorstin, Armand Mastroianni. Story Editors: Sam Hall, Lisa Campanelli, William Gray, M.M. Shelly Moore. Music: Bob Cobert.

Cast. Barnabas Collins: Ben Cross. Roger Collins: Roy Thinnes. Dr. Julia Hoffman: Barbara Steele. Victoria Winters: Joanna Going. Elizabeth Collins: Jean Simmons. Carolyn Stoddard: Barbara Blackburn. David Collins: Joseph Gordon Levitt. Willie Loomis: Jim Fyfe. Josette: Joanna Going. Angelique: Lysette Anthony. Sheriff George Patterson: Michael Cavanaugh. Sarah: Veronica Lauren. Maggie: Ely Pouget.

Dwayne Hickman and Bob Denver in the original "Dobie Gillis"

Dobie Gillis (aka The Many Loves of Dobie Gillis)
CBS (9/29/59–9/18/63)

Dobie (Dwayne Hickman) has married Zelda (Sheila James), has a 16-year-old son Georgie (Steven Paul) and now runs his father Herbert's (Frank

31

Feylen) grocery store. Maynard G. Krebs (Bob Denver) is now a successful entrepreneur and Chatsworth (Steve Franken) has become town banker.

Nearly a decade later, Georgie (Scott Grimes) is *still* a teenager, and following his dad's footsteps in high school with eerie accuracy—he's pursued by the plain Chappie Chatsworth (Tricia Leigh Fisher) but has his heart set on blond, curvaceous Bonnie Bascoe (Lisa Cox). Meanwhile, Dobie has big problems of his own. The town is in the midst of a serious financial crisis—all the factories have closed. And Maynard G. Krebs, whom Dobie hasn't seen in twenty years (guess he forgot about the last visit), shows up and has something to do with the closings. When wealthy widow Thalia Menninger (Connie Stevens) returns, though, it all becomes clear.

Maynard is an innocent dupe. It seems Thalia rescued Maynard from an uncharted desert isle and hired him to buy the firms and plunge the city into bankruptcy so she could perpetrate her evil plot. She plans to offer to reopen the factories and pay all the townspeople $10,000 if Dobie Gillis will divorce Zelda and marry her. Thalia has had several miserable but financially rewarding marriages, but no love.

When Dobie refuses, she is a woman scorned—she offers to give everyone $50,000 if Dobie is killed. Dobie fakes his own death and teaches Thalia, and the townspeople, an important lesson.

"Whatever Happened to Dobie Gillis?"

ABC pilot. 30 minutes (5/10/77). Production Company: Komack Company. Directors: James Komack, Gary Shimokawa. Executive Producers: James Komack, Paul Mason. Producer: Michael Manheim. Writers: Peter Meyerson, Nick Arnold. Creator: Max Schulman.

Cast. Dobie Gillis: Dwayne Hickman. Maynard G. Krebs: Bob Denver. Zelda Gilroy: Sheila James. Herbert T. Gillis: Frank Feylen.

Chatsworth Osbourne: Steve Franken. Georgie Gillis: Steven Paul. Lucky: Lorenzo Lamas. Henshaw: Irwin Wynn. Mrs. Lazlo: Alice Backes. Mrs. Tucker: Susan Davis.

"Bring Me the Head of Dobie Gillis" with Bob
Denver, Dwayne Hickman, and Sheila James.

"Bring Me the Head of Dobie Gillis"

CBS TV movie. Two hours (2/21/88). Production Company: 20th
Century-Fox Television. Director: Stanley Z. Cherry. Executive Producer:
Stanley Z. Cherry. Producers: Dwayne Hickman, Stan Hough, Marc
Summers, Steve Clements. Writers: Deborah Zoe Dawson, Victoria
Johns, Stanley Z. Cherry. From a story by Max Schulman. Creator:
Max Schulman. Music: Jimmy Haskell. Theme: Lionel Newman, Max
Schulman.

Cast. Dobie Gillis: Dwayne Hickman. Zelda Gillis: Sheila James.
Maynard G. Krebs: Bob Denver. Chatsworth Osborne, Jr.: Steve Franken.
Georgie Gillis: Scott Grimes. Thalia Menninger: Connie Stevens. Leander
Pomfritt: William Schallert. Bonnie Bascoe: Lisa Cox. Chatsworth Osborne
III: Tricia Leigh Fisher. Also: Mike Jolly, Nicholas Worth, Kathleen Freeman,
Joey D. Vieira, Dody Goodman, Hank Rolike, James Staley, Lisa Fuller,
William Adams, Janet Rotblatt, Molly David, Billy Beck.

LEE GOLDBERG

Dragnet
NBC (12/16/51–9/6/59)

In 1966, Sgt. Joe Friday (Jack Webb) was still methodically tracking down criminals, only now he had a new partner, Officer Bill Gannon (Harry Morgan), and faced new dilemmas posed by the hippie movement and the drug culture.

Joe Friday stayed with the force until his death while Gannon rose up the ranks to captain, briefly commanding Friday's too-straight and not-too-bright nephew (Dan Aykroyd), who has modeled his life after his much-admired uncle, and his irreverent partner (Tom Hanks).

By 1990, even Gannon has retired, but the LAPD marches on relentlessly in its pursuit and apprehension of those who break the law. Two new officers, Sgt. Vic Daniels (Jeff Osterhage) and Hispanic Sgt. Carl Molina (Bernard White), carry on the Joe Friday tradition of methodical law enforcement.

Background

The 1966 revival pitted ultra-conservative Joe Friday against the liberal counter-culture movement, and the conflict made for some genuine, albeit unintended, fun. It was this show that introduced one generation to Jack Webb's police icon. Television cop shows hadn't changed much in the seven years since "Dragnet" had been canceled, and the revival didn't seem all that out of place–in fact, it was every bit as good as the original series, though a bit more preachy at times.

In 1987, Harry Morgan reprised his role of Bill Gannon (now a captain) in Universal's big-budget theatrical comedy *Dragnet*, with Dan Aykroyd doing an on-target satire of Jack Webb's now famous portrayal of straitlaced, "just the facts, ma'am" Joe Friday. It was, in many ways, a more loyal continuation of "Dragnet" than the next incarnation.

The 1990 Universal syndicated series "The New Dragnet," played straight and done on the cheap by the Arthur Company, was in production simultaneously with "The New Adam-12," and used the same creative staff. The series captured none of the staccato dialogue and unique appeal of the original series. Instead, viewers were subjected to cardboard characters in cardboard stories enacted on cardboard sets. Jeff Osterhage did the narration à la Jack Webb; Efrem Zimbalist, Jr. did the opening and closing narration.

Universal seemingly tackled "The New Dragnet" with blinders on. The realism and edge of such post-"Dragnet" series as "NYPD," "Kojak," "Police Story," and "Hill Street Blues" consigned Jack Webb's almost propagandistic depiction of police officers to history, a humorous anachronism to be enjoyed in its proper context. To tackle such an anachronism straight, and in a contemporary setting, invited ridicule and viewer incredulity, if not boredom, and that's exactly what the series received.

In 2003, ABC turned to Dick Wolf, creator of "Law & Order," to reboot "Dragnet" for a new generation. Ed O'Neill was cast as Joe Friday and Ethan Embry as his partner, Frank Smith. The show had all of the realism of "Law & Order," and the same "ripped from the headlines" story telling, but failed to catch on with viewers. In a desperate attempt to save the show, Wolf brought in a new showrunners, retitled the show "L.A. Dragnet," fired Embry, and paired Friday up with a team of young cops (that included Eva Longoria). The revamp failed and the ax fell in 2004.

"Dragnet"

NBC series. 30 minutes, 98 episodes (1/12/67–9/10/70). Production Company: Universal Television, Mark VII Ltd. Producer: Jack Webb. Creator: Jack Webb. Music: Lyn Murray, Frank Comstock, Stanley Wilson. Theme: Walter Schumann.

Cast. Sgt. Joe Friday: Jack Webb. Off. Bill Gannon: Harry Morgan.

"The New Dragnet"

Syndicated. 30 minutes, 44 episodes (1990). Production Company: Universal Television, The Arthur Company. Executive Producers: Arthur Annecharico, Craig Kellem, Burton Armus. Producer: John Whitman. Story Editors: Joseph Gunn, E. Nick Alexander.

Cast. Sgt. Vic Daniels: Jeff Osterhage. Sgt. Carl Molina: Bernard White. Capt. Lussen: Don Stroud.

Ethan Embry and Ed O'Neill in the 2003 version of "Dragnet"

"Dragnet" aka "L.A. Dragnet"

ABC series. 60 minutes, 22 episodes (2/3/03-5/5/04). Production Company: Universal Television, Wolf Films. Executive Producers: Dick Wolf, Waylon Green. Josh Pate. Jonas Pate. Jeffrey Weiner. Kevin Hooks. Stephen Nathan. Producer: Tim DeLuca. Tyler Bensinger, Billy Fox. Roz Weinman. Robert Nathan. Gary M. Strangis. Peter Jankowski. Barry M. Berg. Arthur W. Forney. Music: Mike Post, Atli Ovarsson

Cast. Lt. Joe Friday: Ed O'Neill. Det. Frank Smith: Ethan Embry. Det. Jimmy McCarron: Desmond Harrington. Det. Gloria Duran: Eva Longoria. Det. Raymond Cooper: Evan Parke. Elana Macias: Roselyn Sanchez. ADA Sandy Chang: Christina Chang. Sanjay Ramachandran: Erick Avari. Det. Hubbel: Katherine Hamhi.

Dynasty
ABC (1/12/81–5/11/89)

When we last saw the Carringtons and the Colbys, each of their lives was at a dangerous precipice. Blake Carrington had killed a corrupt policeman and had been critically wounded himself. His comatose wife Krystle had been committed to a sanitarium. His ex-wife and arch-rival Alexis toppled over a balcony with her lover Dex. And, in secret tunnels beneath the Carrington estate, his daughters Fallon and Krystina were trapped in a cave-in along with a fortune in stolen Nazi art treasures.

Well, Krystle Carrington (Linda Evans) has awakened, and has been spending several long years in a Swiss sanitarium, unknowingly being brainwashed to kill her husband Blake Carrington (John Forsythe), who has just been released from prison and is ready to take on an evil cartel headed by Jeremy Van Dorn (Jeroen Krabbe), who has joined forces with Alexis (Joan Collins) (who survived her fall to head her own fashion business) to destroy what little is left of the Carrington empire.

Background

Viewers were left hanging after "Dynasty" was canceled and its cliffhanger ending was unresolved. Pitting the long-delayed "Dynasty" finale against the World Series may have seemed like a kamikaze mission, but the miniseries was a ratings home run anyway.

"Dynasty: The Reunion"

ABC TV movie. Two parts, four hours (10/20/91 & 10/22/91). Production Company: Richard & Esther Shapiro Productions, Aaron Spelling Productions. Director: Irving J. Moore. Executive Producers: Aaron Spelling, Douglas S. Cramer, Richard and Esther Shapiro, E. Duke Vincent. Producer: Elaine Rich. Writers: Richard and Esther Shapiro, Edward DeBlasio, Robert and Eileen Pollock. Creators: Richard and Esther Shapiro. Music: Peter Myers, Bill Conti.

Cast. Blake Carrington: John Forsythe. Krystle Carrington: Linda Evans. Alexis Carrington: Joan Collins. Fallon Carrington: Emma Samms. Jeff Colby: John James. Miles: Maxwell Caulfield. Steven Carrington: Al Corley. Sammy Jo: Heather Locklear. Jeremy Van Dorn: Jeroen Krabbe. Arlen Marshall: Michael Brandon. Dr. Jobinet: Tony Jay. Adam: Robin Sachs. Krystina: Jessica Player.

The Bradford clan in a 1979 episode: Connie Needham and Willie Aames (front); Dick Van Patten, Betty Buckley, and Adam Rich (middle); and Dianne Kay, Lani O'Grady, Joan Prather, Grant Goodeve, Susan Richardson, Brian Patrick Clarke, and Laurie Walters (rear).

Eight Is Enough
ABC (3/15/77–8/29/81)

The whole family gets together for Tom Bradford's fiftieth birthday, and they all bring their troubles along with them. Tom (Dick Van Patten) has been promoted to editor of the newspaper where he once wrote a column, while his wife Abby, who gained plenty of experience cooking for their huge brood, now runs her own restaurant. But the newspaper is in trouble, and it looks like Tom could be out of work.

David (Grant Goodeve), the eldest, has divorced his longtime love Janet and has given up the construction business for a career as an architect. Mary (Lani O'Grady) achieved her dream of becoming a doctor, and is married to a physician (Jonathan Perpich). Joanie (Laurie Walters) has given up television journalism in favor of acting and has even married a French director (Paul

Rosilli). Nancy (Dianne Kay) and her husband Jeb (Christopher McDonald) are sheep ranchers. Susan (Susan Richardson), who runs a day-care center, and her husband Merle (Brian Patrick Clarke), a high school coach, now have a daughter named Sandy (Amy Gibson). Elizabeth (Connie Needham) and her husband Mark (Peter Nelson) make a living restoring classic cars while Tommy (Willie Aames) struggles as a lounge singer. And if that doesn't make you feel old, pint-sized Nicholas (Adam Rich) is now in college.

The Bradfords overcome their individual troubles and pool together to buy out the newspaper.

Two years later, the family reunites for the marriage of David to his second wife, Marilyn Fulbright (Nancy Everhard), a divorced mother of two small children. The Bradford women aren't wild about this, and they try to drive a wedge between David and Marilyn in the hopes that he will reunite with his ex-wife Janet (Joan Prather). Meanwhile, Tommy has become a sleazy, abrasive, dishonest, talent manager and Nicholas has lost his scholarship due to bad grades, partying, and lousy class attendance. But in the usual Bradford fashion, they solve their problems, the Bradford girls come to love Marilyn, and the wedding goes on.

Background

Mary Frann replaced Betty Buckley as Abby Bradford in the enormously successful "Eight Is Enough Reunion," and Sandy Faison replaced her, in turn, for the less successful "Eight Is Enough Wedding."

"Eight Is Enough: A Family Reunion"

NBC TV movie. Two hours (10/18/87), Production Company: Lorimar Television. Director: Harry Harris. Executive Producer: William Blinn. Producer: Frank Fischer. Writer: Gwen Dubov.

Cast. Tom Bradford: Dick Van Patten. Abby Bradford: Mary Frann. David Bradford: Grant Goodeve. Mary: Lani O'Grady. Joanie: Laurie Walters. Nancy: Dianne Kay. Elizabeth: Connie Needham. Susan: Susan Richardson. Nicholas Bradford: Adam Rich. Tommy Bradford: Willie Aames. Chuck: Jonathan Perpich. Jean-Pierre: Paul Rosilli. Mark: Peter Nelson. Sandy: Amy Gibson.

The cast, reassembled almost intact, for 1989's
"An Eight Is Enough Wedding,"

"An Eight Is Enough Wedding"

NBC TV movie. Two hours (10/5/89). Production Company: Lorimar Television. Director: Stan Nathan. Producer: Greg Strangis. Writer: Greg Strangis. Music: Billy Thorpe.

   Cast. Tom Bradford: Dick Van Patten. Abby Bradford: Sandy Faison. David Bradford: Grant Goodeve. Mary: Lani O'Grady. Joanie: Laurie Walters. Nancy: Dianne Kay. Elizabeth: Connie Needham. Susan: Susan Richardson. Nicholas Bradford: Adam Rich. Tommy Bradford: Willie Aames. Chuck: Jonathan Perpich.

Jean-Pierre: Paul Rosilli. Mark: Peter Nelson. Sandy: Amy Gibson. Marilyn Fulbright: Nancy Everhard. Janet: Joan Prather. Mr. Fulbright: Eugene Roche.

Father Knows Best
CBS (10/3/54–3/27/55)
NBC (8/31/55–9/17/58)
CBS (9/22/58–9/17/62)

Jim and Margaret Anderson (Robert Young & Jane Wyatt) mark their 35th anniversary and everyone comes back together for the celebration. Betty (Elinor Donahue) is now a widow with two kids, Jenny (Cari Anne Warder) and Ellen (Kyle Richards); Bud (Billy Gray) is a motorcycle racer, with a wife (Susan Adams) and a young son (Christopher Gardner); and Kathy (Lauren Chapin) is single but dating a doctor (Hal England) who is ten years older than she is. It's a happy time. But when the holidays roll around, Jim and Margaret find themselves depressed at the prospect of spending the holidays alone and the very real possibility that they have to give up their home.

"Father Knows Best Reunion"

NBC TV movie. 90 minutes (5/15/77). Production Company: Columbia Pictures Television. Director: Norman Abbott. Producer: Hugh Benson. Writer: Paul West.

Cast. Jim Anderson: Robert Young. Margaret Anderson: Jane Wyatt. Betty Anderson: Elinor Donahue. Bud Anderson: Billy Gray. Kathy Anderson: Lauren Chapin. Dr. Jason Harper: Hal England. Frank Carlson: Jim McMullan. Jean: Susan Adams. Jenny: Cari Anne Warder. Robbie Anderson: Christopher Gardner. Ellen: Kyle Richards. Mary Beth: Nellie Bellflower. Reverend Lockwood: Noel Conlon.

"Father Knows Best: Home for Christmas"

NBC TV movie. 90 minutes (12/18/77). Production Company: Columbia Pictures Television. Director: Marc Daniels. Executive Producer: Rene Valentee. Producer: Hugh Benson. Writer: Paul West.

Cast. Jim Anderson: Robert Young. Margaret Anderson: Jane Wyatt. Betty: Elinor Donahue. Kathy: Lauren Chapin. Bud: Billy Gray. Dr. Jason Harper: Hal England. Frank Carlson: Jim McMullan. Jean: Susan Adams. Jenny: Cari Anne Warder. Robbie Anderson: Christopher Gardner. Ellen: Kyle Richards. George Newman: Stuart Lancaster. Jane Newman: June Whitly Taylor. Louise: Priscilla Morrill.

Get Smart
NBC (9/18/65–9/13/69)
CBS (9/26/69–9/11/70)

Max's old employer CONTROL has been abolished, and Max is now a State Department protocol officer, while his wife 99 works on her soon-to-be-published memoir "Out of Control–The Amazing and True Story of America's Most Glamorous Spy." But when KAOS threatens the world with a weather machine, Smart is called out of retirement, along with Hymie (now a crash dummy) and Larabee (who has never left the abandoned CONTROL headquarters) by secret service leader Commander Drury (Kenneth Mars) to stop evil Siegfried (Bernie Kopell), who himself was called out retirement when KAOS was taken over by a corporate raider. The new head of KAOS turns out to be 99's publisher (Harold Gould), who hopes to make the weather so inhospitable that people will stay indoors and be forced, because of bad television reception, to read his books.

Six years later, Max is running CONTROL, Agent 99 is a U.S. Senator and their son Zach (Andy Dick) is now a spy very much in his father's footsteps...teamed up with a female agent, Agent 66 (Elaine Hendrix), to continue the fight against KAOS.

Background
In 1980, Don Adams returned in a theatrical film aimed at launching a series of "Get Smart" movies. In the film, a box office bomb, CONTROL has been abolished, and Smart (a bachelor) now works for Provisional Intelligence Tactical Service (PITS) but is still battling KAOS and its evil plot to make the world nude. Yes, nude. The only other original cast member to appear was Robert Karvelas as Larabee. The movie aired on NBC as "The Return of Maxwell Smart," and was far superior to the 1989 ABC follow-up, "Get Smart, Again!," which did at least reunite all the

surviving cast members (Edward Platt, the original chief, had died some years earlier) for a true extension of the original series. It fared poorly in the ratings, however. But that didn't doom efforts to revive the show. "Get Smart" was brought back again on Fox in 1995 for a mercifully short-lived eight episodes. A movie version of the series, starring Steve Carrell as Maxwell Smart, Anne Hathaway as Agent 99, Alan Arkin as The Chief, and Terence Stamp as Siegfried, was released in 2008.

Don Adams in "The Nude Bomb" is well heeled in
the use of communication equipment.

"The Nude Bomb" (aka "The Return of Maxwell Smart")

Universal Pictures. Theatrical release (1980). Director: Clive Donner. Producer: Jennings Lang. Writers: Arne Sultan, Bill Dana, Leonard B. Stern, based on characters created by Mel Brooks, Buck Henry. Music: Lalo Schifrin.

Cast. Don Adams, Dana Elcar, Sylvia Kristel, Rhonda Fleming, Vittorio Gassman, Pamela Hensley, Vito Scotti, Robert Karvelas, Earl Maynard, Norman Lloyd, Richard Sanders, Byron Webster, Gary Imhoff, Sarah Rush.

Barbara Feldon and Don Adams in "Get Smart, Again!"

"Get Smart, Again!"

ABC TV movie. Two hours (2/26/89). Production Company: Phoenix Entertainment Group, Indieprod Co. Director: Gary Nelson. Executive Producers: Leonard B. Stern, Daniel Melnick. Supervising Producer: Bruce J. Sallan. Producer: Burt Nodella. Writers: Leonard B. Stern, Mark Curtis, Rod Ash. From a story by Leonard B. Stern. Creators: Mel Brooks, Buck Henry. Music: Peter Melnick. Theme: Irving Szathmary.

Cast. Maxwell Smart: Don Adams. Agent 99: Barbara Feldon. Commander Drury: Kenneth Mars. Siegfried: Bernie Kopell. Hymie the

Robot: Dick Gautier. Larabee: Robert Karvelas. Agent 13: Dave Ketchum. Maj. Preston Waterhouse: John de Lancie. Shtarker: King Moody. Dimenti: Harold Gould. Dr. Denton: Danny Goldman. Hottentot: Roger Price. Lisa: Michelle Carson. Dr. Godivar: Kate Stern. Merriweather: Jim Antonio.

"Get Smart"

Fox Series. 30 minutes. (1/15/95-2/19/95) Executive Producers: Vic Kaplan, Lawrence Gay. Michael diGaetano. Leonard B. Stern, Producers: Gary Apple, Nick Marck, Leo J. Clarke. Creators: Mel Brooks, Buck Henry. Music: James Covell. Theme: Irving Szathmary.

Cast. Maxwell Smart: Don Adams. Agent 99: Barbara Feldon. Zach Smart: Andy Dick. Agent 66: Elaine Hendrix. Trudy: Heather Morgan.

Gidget
ABC (9/15/65–9/1/66)

Frances "Gidget" Griffin may be an adult now, married to Jeff "Moondoggie" Griffin (Dean Butler) and running her own travel agency, but she's still the eternal surfing teen of the 1960s. Even Moondoggie, a city planner, still has sand between his toes. It doesn't help that Gidget's niece Danni, is as irrepressible as Gidget was and keeps them all busy at the beach, along with Gidget's retired father (William Schallert).

Background
Following the cancellation of the original "Gidget," there were a number of ill-fated and unrelated television movie pilots attempting to launch a new series. "The New Gidget" was the first direct continuation of the Sally Field series, beginning in 1985 with "Gidget's Summer Reunion," a high-rated, made-for-syndication television movie. The low-budget syndicated series followed, and managed to capture the feel of a genuine 60s sitcom, largely because it was helmed by the since deceased Harry Ackerman, who supervised Screen Gems productions (later bought out by Columbia

Pictures Television) during its heyday when it churned out "Bewitched," "Gidget," "The Flying Nun," "Hazel," and "Dennis the Menace," among others.

Ackerman saw "Gidget" through the Sally Field era of the '60s, the numerous television movies of the '70s, and finally the "New Gidget" of the '80s. "I enjoy it, and I think I add a sense of continuity."

He believed many of the comedies made for first-run syndication were revivals of old series "because distributors want to play it safe for now." Revivals are popular with viewers because "there's an enormous audience appetite for the kind of wholesome family comedy that has been overlooked by the networks and producers in recent times. They have devoted themselves almost exclusively to three-camera audience comedies and are inclined to go more for the fast joke than the character relationships shows like 'Gidget' developed."

The new generation of network executives and sitcom producers, he believed, doesn't know how to do the kind of shows Ackerman did, even though most were raised on them.

"It's quite astounding. In considering writers for 'The New Gidget,' we couldn't find many people who had experience with one-camera shows. It's not a lost art, but it's one that has to be rediscovered by an awful lot of writers."

He originally took the idea of reviving "Gidget" to CBS, which rejected the idea "as too old-fashioned," he said. By then, though, Columbia was "so involved in it, they decided to go ahead with it anyway. It's a timeless character. She has some magic for every generation."

"The New Gidget"

Syndicated. 30 minutes, 44 episodes (1986–88). Executive Producer: Harry Ackerman. Producers: Ralph Riskin, Carole J. Coates, Larry Molin.

Cast. Gidget Griffin: Caryn Richman. Jeff Moondoggie Griffin: Dean Butler. Danni Collins: Sydney Penny. Russ Lawrence: William Schallert. Gail Baker: Lili Haydn. Laurie Powell: Jill Jacobson. Great Kahuna: Don Stroud. Wilton Parmenter: Richard Paul. Karen: Krista Errickson. Julie: Eve LaRue.

The castaways in "Rescue from Gilligan's Island."

Gilligan's Island
CBS (9/26/64–9/3/67)

The seven stranded castaways—Gilligan, the Skipper, the Howells, Ginger, the Professor and Mary Ann—are still living in huts and eating coconuts. But then a Soviet spy satellite crashes on the island, and the Professor is able to use some of its components to fix the *Minnow*'s barometer…in time to discover a massive tidal wave is coming. So our hapless castaways turn their huts into a boat and lash themselves to it. The boat is carried out by the tidal wave and into shipping lanes…and after 15 years, the castaways are finally rescued.

They are greeted in Hawaii by cheering crowds, network newsmen, sailing ships, marching bands, telegrams from the president and the governor, and evil Soviet agents. What do the Russkies want? A super-secret storage disk from the satellite which Gilligan is wearing around his neck. The castaways separate but agree to get together for a Christmas reunion cruise. The Skipper starts fixing up a new cruise boat, the *Minnow II*, but discovers the insurance company won't compensate him for the first boat's loss unless he can get his fellow castaways to sign affidavits that the shipwreck wasn't his fault.

So the Skipper and Gilligan go to visit their friends—while evading the bad guys. Ginger wastes no time getting back into the movies, but finds times have changed—and that now she is expected to do nude scenes. Rather than undress, she wallops the director. The Professor is back in his lab, but finds himself inventing things that have already been invented. The Howells are entertaining guests, and realize the rich have become even snobbier than they are. And Mary Ann is about to marry her fiancé—who has waited for her all these years. The problem is Mary Ann really doesn't want to go through with it. So the Skipper and Gilligan whisk her away from the altar—and themselves from the clutches of those pesky enemy agents.

The insurance company placated, the castaways reunite on the Skipper's new boat and, after catching the Russkies and giving them to the FBI, take a reunion cruise only to get caught in a storm and become shipwrecked on the same uncharted desert isle where they spent the last 15 years.

In all those years, they never discovered what they stumble on now after only a week back on the island—the wreckage of two military airplanes in the jungle. Using parts from both airplanes, the Professor is able to make a working aircraft, and the castaways fly to safety strapped to the wings.

Once ashore, the Howells use their vast wealth to turn Gilligan's Island into a resort paradise hotel—with no phones, no lights, no motorcars, not a single luxury. The resort is dubbed The Castaways, after all the equal partners who will now run the resort with the help of Howell's snobby son, Thurston Howell IV. Now the castaways help others enjoy their vacations and, in many cases, work out problems in their personal lives. And they seem to relish their roles as hosts.

But little do they know that soon a mad scientist, his mad wife, and his mad robots will discover a new energy source on the island, called Supremium, which they need to conquer the world. The castaways foil the plot with the help of the Harlem Globetrotters, who crash land on the island. The mad scientist systematically tricks all the castaways into signing over their deeds to the island. It's up to the Globetrotters to win them back in a basketball challenge with the evil villain's team of evil robot dribblers. But when the

Globetrotters fumble, it is Gilligan who saves the day, stuffing the ball (and himself) into the basket. Gilligan has saved the island, and perhaps the world, from an early demise.

Background

"Rescue from Gilligan's Island" was the surprise smash hit of the 1978–79 season (30.4 rating/52 share), prompting a rash of series revivals that continued virtually unabated through 1986, when the success of "Perry Mason Returns" (27.2/39) sparked a whole new wave of resurrections. "Castaways from Gilligan's Island" was intended to launch a "Love Boat"-esque series about lovers who stay at the resort hotel. "Harlem Globetrotters on Gilligan's Island" was originally intended to feature the Dallas Cowboy cheerleaders.

Perhaps the only revival that approached the phenomenal popular success of "Rescue from Gilligan's Island" was another Sherwood Schwartz production, "A Very Brady Christmas," a decade later, scoring an incredible 25.1/39 to singlehandedly boost CBS into second place the week it aired.

"Rescue from Gilligan's Island"

NBC TV movie (10/14–15/78). Production Company: Redwood Productions, Paramount Television. Executive Producer: Sherwood Schwartz. Director: Leslie H. Martinson. Producer: Lloyd Schwartz. Writers: Sherwood Schwartz, Elroy Schwartz, Al Schwartz, David Harmon.

Cast. Gilligan: Bob Denver. The Skipper: Alan Hale, Jr. Thurston Howell: Jim Backus. Mrs. Howell: Natalie Schafer. Ginger: Judith Baldwin. The Professor: Russell Johnson. Mary Ann: Dawn Wells. Dimitri: Vincent Schiavelli. Miss Ainsworth: June Whitley Taylor. Butler: Martin Ashe.

"Castaways on Gilligan's Island"

NBC TV movie (5/3/79). Production Company: Redwood Productions, Paramount Television. Executive Producer: Sherwood Schwartz. Director:

Earl Bellamy. Producer: Lloyd Schwartz. Writers: Sherwood Schwartz, Elroy Schwartz, Al Schwartz.

Cast. Gilligan: Bob Denver. The Skipper: Alan Hale, Jr. Thurston Howell: Jim Backus. Mrs. Howell: Natalie Schafer. Ginger: Constance Forslund. The Professor: Russell Johnson. Mary Ann: Dawn Wells. Thurston Howell IV: David Ruprecht. Henry Elliot: Tom Bosley. Myra Elliot: Marcia Wallace. Robbie: Ronnie Scribner. Tom Larson: Rod Browning.

"Harlem Globetrotters on Gilligan's Island"

NBC TV movie (5/15/81). Production Company: Redwood Production, Paramount Television. Executive Producer: Sherwood Schwartz. Director: Peter Baldwin. Producer: Lloyd Schwartz. Writers: Sherwood Schwartz, Al Schwartz, David P. Harmon, Gordon Mitchell.

Cast. Gilligan: Bob Denver. The Skipper: Alan Hale Jr. Thurston Howell: Jim Backus. Mrs. Howell: Natalie Schafer. Ginger: Constance Forslund. The Professor: Russell Johnson. Mary Ann: Dawn Wells. Thurston Howell IV: David Ruprecht. Lucinda: Dreama Denver. Manager: Rosalind Chao. J.J. Pierson: Martin Landau. Olga Schmetner: Barbara Bain. Dewey Stevens: Scatman Crothers. Sportscaster: Chick Hearn.

See also "New Adventures of Gilligan" and "Gilligan's Planet" in the appendix.

The Greatest American Hero
ABC (3/18/81–2/3/83)

Schoolteacher Ralph Hinkley (William Katt), who was given a superhero suit endowed with special powers by benevolent aliens, is still fighting crime with the help of his lawyer girlfriend (Connie Selleca) and hard-boiled FBI agent Bill Maxwell (Robert Culp)—that is, until he is finally unmasked to the public. Now that everyone knows he is a superhero, the aliens erase mankind's memory and give the suit to a young woman (Mary Ellen Stuart), also a school teacher and a foster parent (to Mya

Akerling), and she resumes the good fight, teamed with reluctant partner Bill Maxwell.

Background

A demonstration film aimed at sparking a revamped version of the ABC series "The Greatest American Hero" for the Sunday evening 7–8 PM time slot (that eventually went to "Our House").

The demo, culled from a two-hour script by Babs Greyhosky, teamed Robert Culp as FBI Agent Bill Maxwell with 25-year-old Mary Ellen Stuart, who Greyhosky says plays a character who is a "save the everything type who runs a day-care center." Stewart gets the superhero suit that aliens originally bestowed on Ralph Hinkley (William Katt).

Ralph is exposed to the world as a superhero and "goes on talk shows and gets an attitude," says Greyhosky, so the aliens "make the world forget him."

The revival came about when executive producer/creator Stephen J. Cannell attended a celebration in honor of his unveiled star on Hollywood Boulevard. Clips of his past and present shows were screened as part of the presentation, prompting then-NBC President Brandon Tartikoff to lean over and tell him, "ABC made a big mistake canceling that show," according to Cannell, who responded, "How about doing the show again?"

However, Tartikoff didn't like the show enough to order a new version. The unaired demo film was later combined with excerpts from previous episodes, dubbed "Greatest American Heroine," and added to the syndication package.

"The Greatest American Heroine"

NBC pilot. 20 minutes, unaired (1989). Production Company: Stephen J. Cannell Productions. Director: Tony Mordente. Executive Producers: Stephen J. Cannell, Babs Greyhosky. Producer: Jo Swerling, Jr. Writer: Babs Greyhosky. Creator: Stephen J. Cannell. Music: Mike Post, Pete Carpenter.

Cast. Ralph Hinkley: William Katt. Pamela Davidson: Connie Selleca. Bill Maxwell: Robert Culp. Holly Hathaway: Mary Ellen Stuart.

Green Acres
cbs (9/15/65–9/7/71)

Hooterville seems to have been frozen in time—for the most part. Fred and Doris Ziffel have passed away, so the farm and Arnold the Pig are now the responsibility of their daughter Daisy (Mary Tanner). And after all these years, the lunacy of the town has finally taken its toll on Oliver (Eddie Albert), who sells out to Mr. Haney (Pat Buttram) and returns with Lisa (Eva Gabor) to her beloved Park Avenue, which they left behind 25 years ago. But when a heartless real estate tycoon (Henry Gibson) attempts to bulldoze the entire town to make way for a parking lot, Oliver returns to Hooterville to defend the town—and in doing so, realizes he can never leave and buys back his farm.

"Return to Green Acres"

CBS TV movie. Two hours (5/18/90). Production Company: Jaygee Productions, Orion Television Entertainment. Director: William Asher. Executive Producer: Jerry Golod. Producer: Anthony Santa Croce. Writers: Craig Heller, Guy Shulman. Based on characters created by Jay Sommers. Theme: Vic Mizzy. Music: Dan Follart.

Cast. Oliver Douglas: Eddie Albert. Lisa Douglas: Eva Gabor. Sam Drucker: Frank Cady. Hank Kimball: Alvy Moore. Alf: Sid Melton. Ralph: Mary Grace Canfield. Eb Dawson: Tom Lester. Mr. Haney: Pat Buttram. Daisy Ziffel: Mary Tanner. E. Mitchell Armstrong: Henry Gibson. Also: John Scott Clough, Mark Ballou, Lucy Lee Flippin, John Asher, Jeff Rochlin, Lycia Naff, John Alvin, Tom Simmons, Sally Kemp, Tippi Hedren, Lisa Figus, Don Perry, Robin Frizzel, John Otrin, Melanie MacQueen, Frank Fowler, Hank Underwood, Santos Morales, T.J. Castronovo, Karen Haber, Michael Sessa, Sam Denoff, David Permenter, Humberto Ortiz, Wayne Chou, Dayton Callie, Stephanie Kaylan, Brian McMillan, Frank Welker.

Gunsmoke
CBS (9/10/55–9/1/75)

Matt Dillon (James Arness) turned in his badge twelve years ago, and has been a mountain man and trapper ever since, leaving Dodge City in the able hands of his former deputy, Newly O'Brien (Buck Taylor). Doc has passed away, and Miss Kitty (Amanda Blake) has sold the Long Branch Saloon to Miss Hannah (Fran Ryan). Dillon may be older and craggier, but he is tougher than ever.

Dillon returns to Dodge City when an old adversary, Will Mannon (Steve Forrest), escapes from jail and comes looking for vengeance and for Miss Kitty. The only way to stop Mannon is to kill him, and Dillon does, despite a near-fatal injury.

Dillon leaves Miss Kitty behind and returns to his solitary life in the hills, only to discover, in a long-delayed letter from old flame Mike Yardner (Michael Learned) that he has a teenage daughter Beth (Amy Stock Poynton)—and that she has been kidnapped by Apaches. Seems that 18 years ago, widow Mike rescued Matt, who had been left injured and stricken with amnesia after an ambush. She brought him back to her farm and they had a romantic interlude. She kept the pregnancy secret because she knew that once Matt remembered who he was, he would go back to his calling—enforcing the law in Dodge City. Now Dillon hits the trail to rescue the daughter he never knew he had and to fight for a chance at a family life he thought he could never have. He overcomes bloodthirsty cavalry, a headstrong Indian, and an unforgiving Mexican wasteland to find Beth and bring her to safety.

Reunited with his daughter and Mike, Dillon settles down to a life on the farm, all the while knowing that his peace is no doubt short-lived, that danger has a way of blowing into his life like sagebrush.

A year later, Mike succumbs to "the fever," and Dillon decides to send Beth to school back East. But those plans change when a bloody vendetta, an offshoot of the war between the Tewksburys and the Grahams in Pleasant Valley, Arizona, is played out on Dillon's ranch. Tommy Graham (Joseph Bottoms) and his gang murder a Tewksbury working for Dillon, and then steal the cattle. Dillon sets out to find the desperados, unaware that stubborn Beth and Will (Matt Mulhern), one of their ranch hands, are following his trail to help him out.

Dillon stumbles onto a bloodthirsty gang of vigilantes, led by powerful rancher Col. Tucker (Pat Hingle), who are hanging anyone they suspect is a criminal. Meanwhile, Beth and Will seek shelter from a storm with some friendly ranchers who turn out to be Tewksburys, and who are slaughtered in cold blood by Tommy Graham. Beth and Will survive thanks to Matt Dillon, who shows up at just the right time.

Dillon takes it upon himself to hunt down Graham and bring him in, alive or dead. Dillon ends up dragging in a corpse to the local sheriff (Morgan Woodward), a man who long ago turned a blind eye to the troubles in his territory. When an innocent boy is hanged, he and Dillon set out together to stop the vigilantes and clean up the territory.

Matt Dillons returns to his ranch, ready to settle down as a cowboy and watch the romance that is sure to bloom between Will and Beth. But he ends up getting involved in more trouble…

Background

The "Gunsmoke" revivals were class acts, easily among the best TV continuations ever made. They were every bit as good as the TV series and depicted a version of Matt Dillon clearly shaped by all the experiences he'd had before. They were top-notch productions on every level and initially featured scripts written by "Gunsmoke" veterans. But there was a bittersweet quality to the movies. Although the first two picked up on narrative threads from the series, this wasn't the "Gunsmoke" we knew. Dillon wasn't a U.S. Marshal any more. He was an aging fur trapper. And after the first movie, he never returned to Dodge City again, which was a shame. It would have been nice to see Festus, Chester or Newly again (the deaths of Milburn Stone, who played Doc, and Amanda Blake, who played Miss Kitty, made their reappearances impossible). As great as the movies were, by the time the fifth, and weakest, one ended, Dillon was far too old to be credible as a gunfighter. The final "Gunsmoke" movie marked Arness' final role.

"Gunsmoke: Return to Dodge"

CBS TV movie (9/26/87). Production Company: CBS Entertainment. Director: Vincent McEveety. Executive Producer: John Mantley. Writer: Jim Byrnes.

Cast. Matt Dillon: James Arness. Kitty Russell: Amanda Blake. Newly O'Brien: Buck Taylor. Miss Hannah: Fran Ryan. Will Mannon: Steve Forrest. Jake Flagg: Earl Holliman. Lt. Dexter: Ken Olandt. Digger: W. Morgan Sheppard. Bright Water: Patrice Martinez. Little Doe: Tantoo Cardinal. Oakum: Mickey Jones. Logan: Frank M. Totino. Warden Brown: Robert Koons. Judge Collins: Walter Kaasa. Mrs. Collins: George Collins. Farnum: Tony Epper. Bubba: Louie Ellias. Potts: Ken Kirzinger. Clyman: Denny Arnold. The Flogger: Alex Green.

"Gunsmoke II: The Last Apache"

CBS TV movie (3/19/90). Production Company: CBS Entertainment. Director: Charles Correll. Executive Producer: John Mantley. Producer: Stan Hough. Writer: Earl Wallace.

Cast. Matt Dillon: James Arness. Mike Yardner: Michael Learned. Beth Yardner: Amy Stock Poynton. Chalk Brighton: Richard Kiley. Wolf: Joe Lara. Bodine: Geoffrey Lewis. Geronimo: Joaquin Martinez. Lt. Davis: Peter Murnik.

"Gunsmoke III: To the Last Man"

CBS TV movie. Two hours (1/10/92). Production Company: CBS Entertainment. Supervising Producer: Jim Byrnes. Producer: Ken Swor. Director: Jerry Jameson. Writer: Earl W. Wallace. Music: Artie Kane.

Cast. Matt Dillon: James Arness. Col. Tucker: Pat Hingle. Beth Yardner: Amy Stock Poynton. Will McCall: Matt Mulhern. Abel Rose: Morgan Woodward. Rusty Dover: Jason Lively. Tommy Graham: Joseph Bottoms.

Horse Trader: Mills Watson. Zach: James Booth. Lizzie Tewksbury: Amanda Wyss. Deputy Willie Rudd: Jim Beaver. John Tewksbury: Herman Poppe. Charlie Tewksbury: Ken Swofford, Sheriff Tom: Don Collier. Billy Watson: Ed Adams. Claire Oliver: Kathleen Todd. Kirby Tewksbury: Loy W. Burns. Virgil Tucker: Andy Sherman. Rowe Blevin: Clark Ray. Bartender: Michael F. Woodson.

"Gunsmoke IV: The Long Ride"

CBS TV movie. Two hours (5/8/93). Production Company: CBS Entertainment. Executive Producer: James Arness, Norman S. Powell. Supervising Producer: Jim Byrnes. Producer: Ken Swor. Director: Jerry Jameson. Writer: Bill Stratton. Music: Artie Kane.

Cast. Matt Dillon: James Arness. John Parsley: James Brolin, Beth: Amy Stock Poynton. Will: Christopher Bradley. Uncle Jane Merkel: Ali McGraw. Jules Braxton: Don McManus. Deputy Monaghan: Patrick Dollaghan, Collie Whitebird: Marco Sanchez, Sheriff Bart Meriweather: Tim Choate. Ike Berry: Michael Greene. Dr. Strader: Stewart Moss. Traveling Blacksmith: Jim Beaver.

"Gunsmoke V: One Man's Justice"

CBS TV movie. Two hours (2/10/94). Production Company: CBS Entertainment. Director: Jerry Jameson. Executive Producers: James Arness, Norman S. Powell, Jerry Jameson. Producer: Ken Swor. Director: Jerry Jameson. Writer: Harry Longstreet, Renee Longstreet Music: Artie Kane.

Cast. Matt Dillon: James Arness. Davis Healy: Bruce Boxleitner. Lucas Miller: Kelly Morgan. Beth: Amy Stock-Poynton. Sean Devlin: Alan Scarfe, Will: Christopher Bradley. Martin Miller: Mikey LeBeau. Hannah Miller: Hallie Foote. Jesse: Clark Brolly. Sheriff: Don Collier. Waco: Ed Adams. Six Eyes: Apesanahkwat

I Dream of Jeannie
NBC (9/18/65–9/1/70)

Former astronaut Col. Tony Nelson and his wife Jeannie (Barbara Eden), a genuine genie from a bottle, are now parents of a teenage Tony, Jr. (MacKenzie Astin). Unfortunately, not all is well–they are having marital problems as Jeannie asserts her independence, moves out into an apartment of her own, and gets a job in a sporting goods store. Making matters worse is Jeannie's evil twin sister, who does everything she can to drive a wedge between Jeannie and Tony so she can have Tony for herself.

But when Tony is trapped in a malfunctioning space shuttle and facing imminent death in a collision with an asteroid, Jeannie appeals to Hadji, an all-powerful genie, to save her husband, since normal génies can't use their powers to keep others from dying. In return for this favor, Hadji erases all memory of Jeannie and T.J. from Tony's mind. Six months later, however, Jeannie bumps into Tony and their romance begins anew.

Six years later, Col. Nelson is somewhere in deep space on a secret mission, leaving Jeannie and their son Tony, Jr., who remarkably is still a teenager. Jeannie's evil twin sister (Barbara Eden) shows up and informs her that according to genie rules, if a genie goes without a master for three months, she must be banished to Mesopotamia forever. That means Jeannie has to find a temporary master–and fast. Complicating things are her twin sister, who wants to take her place on Earth, and a gang of thieves that Tony, Jr., falls in with.

Background

Larry Hagman, tied up played J.R. Ewing in "Dallas," was replaced by Wayne Rogers in the first revival, and his character was lost in space for the second. "I Dream of Jeannie: Fifteen Years Later," scored against the second game of the World Series, stealing a third of the audience and ranking in the top ten primetime programs of the week. The second revival, some five years later, wasn't as lucky–it was demolished by the World Series and another revival, "Dynasty: The Reunion."

"I Dream of Jeannie: Fifteen Years Later"

NBC TV movie. Two hours (10/20/85). Production Company: Can't Sing, Can't Dance Productions, Columbia Pictures Television. Director: William Asher. Executive Producer: Barbara Corday. Producer: Hugh Benson. Writer: Irma Kalish. From a Story by Dinah Kirgo, Julie Kirgo, and Irma Kalish. Creator: Sidney Sheldon. Music: Mark Snow. Theme by Hugo Montenegro, Buddy Kaye.

Cast. Jeannie: Barbara Eden. Tony Nelson: Wayne Rogers. T.J. Nelson: MacKenzie Astin. Roger Healey: Bill Daily. Dr. Alfred Bellows: Hayden Roarke. Wes Morrison: John Bennett Perry. Scheherazade: Dody Goodman. Nelly Hunt: Lee Taylor Allen. Dori Green: Dori Brenner. Haji: Andre Shields. General Hatten: Michael Fairman. Col. Klapper: Dierk Torsek. Mrs. Farrell: Belita Moreno. Melissa: Nicole Eggert. Millie: Helen J. Siff. Tony, Jr.-Age 7: Brandon Call. Reporter: Bill Shick.

"I Still Dream of Jeannie"

NBC TV movie. Two hours (10/20/91). Production Company: Jeannie Entertainment, Carla Singer Productions, Columbia Pictures Television, Bar-Gene Television. Director: Joseph Scanlan. Executive Producer: Carla Singer. Producer: Joan Carson. Writer: April Kelly. Creator: Sidney Sheldon. Music: Ken Harrison.

Cast. Jeannie: Barbara Eden. Roger Healey: Bill Daily. Tony Nelson, Jr.: Christopher Bolton. Simpson: Ken Kercheval. Sham-Ir: Peter Breck. General Westcott: Al Waxman.

See also "Jeannie" in the appendix.

Eric Kramer (as Thor), Bill Bixby, and Lou Ferrigno
in "The Incredible Hulk Returns."

The Incredible Hulk
CBS (3/10/78–5/19/82)

David Banner is still on the run, trying to "quell the raging beast that dwells within him," and he thinks he may finally be close to a cure. He's working as a lab technician for a huge corporation, exploring gamma radiation and living with a fellow scientist (Lee Purcell). But his plans go awry when anthropology student Donald Blake (Steve Levitt) discovers a magic hammer that conjures up Thor (Eric Kramer), a Viking warrior, and bad guys kidnap Banner's girlfriend. Soon even McGee, the reporter obsessed with capturing the Hulk, is closing in. But Banner, his raging alter ego, and Thor manage to stomp the bad guys, and Banner hits the road again, leaving Thor and Donald Blake to fight crime together.

The road takes David Banner to the big city, where he is falsely accused of a crime and represented by a blind public defender (Rex Smith)—a man who, David discovers, is actually the superhero Daredevil, whose heightened senses and incredible gymnastic skills make him a formidable foe against evil. Together, David and the Daredevil bring down a powerful, criminal mastermind (John Rhys-Davies). And then David hits the road once more.

He pretends to be retarded and finds a job at Genecor Research as a custodian so that he can be near Dr. Ronald Pratt, who is close to a breakthrough in the very gammaradiation gene research that David was doing when he inadvertently unlocked the raging beast within him. What David doesn't know is that a secret espionage organization has assigned its ace spy, a master of disguise named Jasmin (Elizabeth Gracen), to kidnap Dr. Pratt and steal his experiments. Pratt is about to cure David when Jasmin intervenes. Pratt is seriously injured, and David once more is framed for a crime he didn't commit. But when the espionage agency, run by Jasmin's evil sister, tries to kill Jasmin, she and David become unlikely allies—and lovers.

When Pratt and his wife are kidnapped by the evil spy organization, Jasmin and David go to rescue them. In the course of the rescue, David hulks out and, as the green monster, leaps onto the airplane the evil sister is escaping in. The plane goes airborne, there's a fight inside, and the plane explodes. The Hulk plummets to earth and slams into the tarmac. Jasmin arrives at the Hulk's side just as he transforms back into David Banner and dies—finally free of his curse.

Background
New World Pictures and ABC used a revival of "The Incredible Hulk" (CBS, 1978–82) as a ploy to launch "Thor," a proposed series based on the Marvel comic. When that didn't sell, "The Incredible Hulk" was used as a vehicle for the aborted launch of another Marvel character, "Daredevil," and finally, a female spy named "Jasmin." None of them caught on.

"The Incredible Hulk Returns"

NBC TV movie. Two hours (5/22/88). Production Company: New World Television, B&B Productions. Director: Nicholas Corea. Executive Producers: Nicholas Corea, Bill Bixby. Producer: Daniel McPhee. Writer: Nicholas

Corea. Creator: Kenneth Johnson. Based on the Marvel Comics character. Music: Lance Rubin.

Cast. David Banner: Bill Bixby. Hulk: Lou Ferrigno. Jack McGee: Jack Colvin. Donald Blake: Steve Levitt. Thor: Eric Kramer. Maggie Shaw: Lee Purcell. Jack LeBeau: Tim Thomerson. Also: Charles Napier, Eric Kramer, William Riley, Tom Finnegan, Donald Willis, Carl Nick Ciafalio, Bobby Travis McLaughlin, Burke Denis, Nick Costa, Peisha McPhee, William Malone, Joanie Allen.

Bill Bixby in "The Trial of the Incredible Hulk."

"The Trial of the Incredible Hulk"

NBC TV movie. Two hours (5/7/89). Production Company: Bixby-Brandon Productions, New World Television. Director: Bill Bixby. Executive Producers: Bill Bixby, Gerald DiPego. Producers: Hugh Spencer Phillips, Robert Ewing. Writer: Gerald DiPego.

Cast. David Banner: Bill Bixby. Hulk: Lou Ferrigno. Ellie Mendez: Marta DeBois. Christa Klein: Nancy Everhard. Edgar: Nicholas Hormann. Al Pettiman: Richard Cummings, Jr. Tendelli: Joseph Mascolo. Matt Murdock (Daredevil): Rex Smith. Also: John Rhys-Davies, Linda Darlow, John Novak, Dwight Koss, Meredith Woodward, Mark Acheson, Richard Newman, Don MacKay, Doug Abrahams, Mitchell Kosterman, Beatrice Zeilinger.

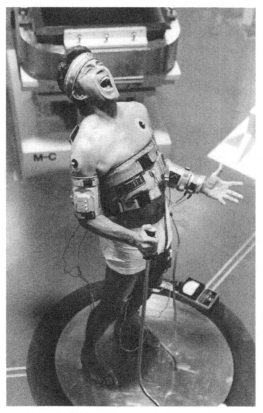

A painful transformation in "The Death of the Incredible Hulk."

"The Death of the Incredible Hulk"

NBC TV movie. Two hours (2/18/90). Production Company: Bixby-Brandon Productions, New World Television. Director: Bill Bixby. Executive Producer: Bill Bixby. Producers: Hugh Spencer Phillips, Robert Ewing. Writer: Gerald DiPego. Music: Lance Rubin.

Cast. David Banner: Bill Bixby. Hulk: Lou Ferrigno. Jasmin: Elizabeth Gracen. Dr. Ronald Pratt: Philip Sterling. Amy Pratt: Barbara Tarbuck. Kasha: Andreas Katsulas. Betty: Chilton Crane. Bank Teller: Carla Ferrigno. Tom: Duncan Fraser. Brenn: Dwight McFee. Crane: Lindsay Bourne. Pauley: Mina E. Mina. Luanne Crane: Marlane O'Brien. Shoup: Garwin Sanford. Dodger: Justin DiPego. Aaron Colmer: Fred Henderson. Carbino: Judith Maxie. George Tilmer: French Tuckner.

The cast of "It's a Living."

It's a Living
ABC (10/30/80–9/10/82)

The trials and tribulations of the staff at the Above the Top restaurant continue. Waitresses Lois Adams (Susan Sullivan), the happily married mother of two; sweet and innocent Vicki Allen (Wendy Schaal); and widow Maggie McBirney (Louise Lasser) are all gone. But there are still some familiar faces. Sharp-tongued Cassie Cranston (Ann Jillian), aspiring actress Dot Higgins (Gail Edwards), and law student and divorced mother Jan Hoffmeyer (Barrie Youngfellow) are still waiting tables. And, of course, haughty, uptight manager Nancy Beebee (Marian Mercer) and obnoxious piano player Sonny Mann (Paul Kreppel) haven't left. Beebee even falls for the new chef, Howard Miller (Richard Stahl) and they get married. When Cassie leaves after several years waiting tables, she's replaced by black waitress Ginger St. James (Sheryl Lee Ralph), who joins the other new faces in the restaurant–waitress Amy Tompkins (Crystal Bernard), a small town girl from Texas trying to make it in the big city, and Frisco (Robyn Petersen), the lady bartender.

Background

"It's a Living" was rocky going from the start, beginning with the title (changed to "Making a Living" then back again for syndication) and on through numerous cast changes during both its network and syndicated runs. It never quite found a following, but it managed to struggle on nonetheless through a hundred episodes, most of them in its second life in first-run syndication.

"It's a Living"

Syndicated. 30 minutes, 100 episodes (1985–89). Production Company: Witt/Thomas Productions, LBS Communications, Lorimar Telepictures. Executive Producers: Paul Junger Witt, Tony Thomas, Bob Colleary. Producers: Tom Whedon, Marc Sotkin. Creators: Stu Silver, Dick Clair, Jenna McMahon. Music: George Tipton. Theme: Leslie Bricusse.

Cast. Cassie Cranston: Ann Jillian. Dot Higgins: Gail Edwards. Jan Hoffmeyer: Barrie Youngfellow. Nancy Beebee: Marian Mercer. Sonny Mann: Paul Kreppel. Ginger St. James: Sheryl Lee Ralph. Amy Topkins: Crystal Bernard. Frisco: Robyn Petersen. Howard Miller: Richard Stahl.

David Hasselhoff in "Knightrider."

Knightrider
NBC (9/26/82–8/8/86)

There are two alternate realities for the way things turned out for Michael Knight after 1986...

In one version, set in the year 2000 (at that point, decades into the future), the world has changed dramatically. Handguns have been outlawed, and cops are carrying stun guns instead. Death sentences have been outlawed, and criminals are no longer given prison sentences—instead, they are put into suspended animation.

Michael Knight (David Hasselhoff) has apparently been in suspended animation as well—he certainly doesn't look like a 50-year-old man. Retirement must have been good for his complexion. He has spent the last decade fishing, and is called out of retirement by Devon (Edward Mulhare), who also seems to have cheated the aging process, to help Knight Industries win a crucial freelance law enforcement contract with the city.

Michael returns to discover that KITT (voice of William Daniels), his talking, crime-fighting car, has been dismantled and sold off for parts by Russ Maddock (Carmen Argenziano), now partnered in Knight Industries with Devon. In fact, some of KITT's essential chips end up in the brain of Shawn McCormick (Megan Butler), a police officer shot in the head and left for dead by corrupt cops who are involved in a handgun importing scheme. What's left of KITT is put into Michael's '57 Chevy.

Shawn is hired by Knight Industries as a new operative, and together with Michael, she takes on the bad guys, who kidnap Devon and kill him. The baddies nearly kill Michael, Shawn, and KITT as well, forcing their car off the road and into the ocean. But our heroes survive, and KITT is transferred into the Knight 4000, a supercar equipped with stun guns, voice imitator, view phone, laser fax machine, and something called an "aromanometer," which can sniff a woman's perfume and identify the brand.

Our heroes bring down the bad guys, and Michael returns to a life of fishing, leaving Shawn, Maddock and KITT to fight for justice…

But in a different reality, one where those events didn't happen, Michael has an affair with a woman named Jennifer Traceur (Susan Gibney) and gets her pregnant. Michael and Jennifer become estranged and she raises their son Mike (Justin Bruening) alone. Mike becomes a U.S. Army ranger, and professional poker player, and falls in love with Sarah Graiman (Deanna Russo), the scientist/daughter of Charles Graiman (Bruce Davison), KITT's creator.

In 2008. Charles is kidnapped and KITT, now installed in a Ford Mustang, seeks out Sarah and Mike. In their efforts to rescue Charles, Mike's mother Jennifer is killed. At Jennifer's funeral, Mike is reunited with his father Michael Knight…who reminds him that "one man can make a difference." This sage, fatherly advice helps convince Mike to join a resurrected Foundation of Law and Government (aka Knight Industries), become KITT's driver, and fight crime with a team of fellow agents, including FBI Special Agent Rivai (Sydney Tamila Poitier). And later, he even changes his name from Traceur to Knight...

Background

The revival movie "Knightrider 2000" was shot on location in San Antonio, Texas and was generally well received by critics...but it fizzled as a pilot.

Universal later rebooted "Knightrider" for a post apocalyptic, "Mad Max"-esque pilot entitled "Knighrider 2010" that went nowhere. Undaunted, Universal launched a first-run syndicated series called "Team Knightrider" about a group of crimefighters with special cars. It had nothing to do with the original series and died after one season.

Finally, in 2008, Doug Liman, the director of "The Bourne Identity" and Gary Scott Thompson, the screenwriter behind the hit movie "The Fast & The Furious," teamed up for a "Knightrider" revival/sequel for NBC that was built around Michael Knight's estranged son and a new, talking car. Hasselhoff made a cameo appearance in the pilot. The movie did so well in the ratings that NBC immediately commissioned a new series. Will Arnett initially voiced KITT in the pilot but was replaced by Val Kilmer before airing. The new series bombed and was off the air in less that one season.

"Knightrider 2000"

NBC TV movie. Two hours (5/19/91). Production Company: Riven River Productions, Universal Television. Director: Alan J. Levi. Executive Producer: Michelle Brustin. Producers: Chuck Sellier, Rob Hedden. Writer: Rob Hedden. Creator: Glen A. Larson. Music: Jan Hammer.

Cast. Michael Knight: David Hasselhoff. Devon: Edward Mulhare. Shawn McCormick: Megan Butler. Russ Maddock: Carmen Argenziano. KITT: William Daniels. Also: Eugene Clark, Mitch Pileggi, Christine Healy, Lou Beatty, Jr., Frances Guinan, John Cannon Nichols, James Doohan.

"Knightrider 2010"

Syndicated. 90 minutes. (2/13/94) Production Company: Universal Television. Director: Sam Pillsbury. Executive Producers: Rob Cohen, John Leekley Producer: Alex Beaton. Writer: John Leekley. Music: Tim Truman

Cast: Jake McQueen: Richard Joseph Paul. Hannah Tyrie: Heidi Leick. Marshal Will McQueen: Michael Beach. Dean: Don McManus. Johnny: Nicky Katt. Zeke: Badja Djola. Robert Lee: Mark Pellegrino. Jared: Brion James.

"Team Knightrider"

Syndicated. 60 minutes. 22 episodes (10/6/97-5/18/98) Production Company: Universal Television. Executive Producers: Rick Copp, David A Goodman. Glen A. Larson. Producers: Gilbert Alexander Wadsworth III, Scott McAboy. Music: Gary Stockdale

Cast: Kyle Stewart: Brixton James. Jenny Andrews: Christine Steel. Duke DePalma: Duane Davis. Erica West: Kathy Trageser. Kevin 'Trek' Sanders: Nick Wechsler. Shadow: Steve Forrest. Dante: Tom Kane. Domino: Nia Vardalos. Beast: Kerrigan Mahan. Plato: John Kassir. Clayton: Rick Copp. Gil: Vince Waldron.

Justin Bruening as Mike Knight in the 2008 version of *Knightrider*

"Knightrider" (The 2008 Pilot)

NBC movie. Two hours. (2/17/2008). Production Company: Universal Television. Dutch Oven. Director: Steve Shill. Executive Producers: Doug

Liman. Dave Bartis. Glen A. Larson. Supervising Producer: David Andron. Producer: Sean Ryerson. Geoff Garrett. Sara Fischer. Writer: David Andron. Music: Christopher Tyng.

Cast: Mike Traceur: Justin Bruening. Jessica Traceur: Susan Gibney. Charles Graiman: Bruce Davison. Sarah Graiman: Deanna Russo. Michael Knight: David Hasselhoff. FBI Agent Carrie Rivai: Sydney Tamilia Poitier. Dylan Fass: Wayne Kasserman. Sheriff Ramsey: Chris Mulkey. Kevin: Jonathan Chase. Belle: Kevin Christy. Cross: Jack Yang. Smoke: Kevin Dunigan. Dustin Carey: Blake Silver. KITT: Val Kilmer

"Knightrider" (The 2008-2009 Series)

NBC series. 60 minutes. 18 episodes (9/24/2008-3/4/2009) Production Company: Universal Television. Executive Producers: Gary Scott Thompson, David Bartis, Matt Pyken, Glen A. Larson, Doug Liman, Rob Wright, Steve Shill Supervising Producer: David Andron, Sean Ryerson. Producers: Sara Fischer, Julie Herlocker, Philip Levens, Patrick Massett, John Zinman, Gavin Barclay, Geoff Garrett. Music: Christopher Tyng

Cast: Mike Traceur: Justin Bruening. Jessica Traceur: Susan Gibney. Charles Graiman: Bruce Davison. Sarah Graiman: Deanna Russo. FBI Agent Carrie Rivai: Sydney Tamilia Poitier. Dylan Fass: Wayne Kasserman. KITT: Val Kilmer.

Kojak
cbs (10/24/73–4/15/78)

Lt. Theo Kojak (Telly Savalas) is still a tough NYPD detective bucking bureaucrats while bearing down on his hard-working staff, which once again includes Stavros (George Savalas), Rizzo (Vince Conti) and Saperstein (Mark B. Russell). Even Capt. McNeil (Dan Frazer) shows up. Crocker has left the department to pursue a career in politics. Kojak's friend (Max Von Sydow) may be involved in the murders of three suspected Nazi war criminals living in

New York. Kojak bucks department orders to butt out and becomes involved with a state department official (Suzanne Pleshette) who helps him obtain crucial information–contained in the so-called Belarus file–that the agency won't reveal.

Despite irritating his superiors, Kojak is nonetheless promoted to inspector, heading a NYPD major crime unit and leaving his old team of detectives behind. One of his first cases is the investigation of charges that a woman (Kate Nelligan) murdered her children while they slept. Kojak enlists the aid of his new protégé, Det. Bass (John Bedford-Lloyd), to unravel the mystery.

A few years later, Inspector Kojak has a new protégé, Det. Blake (Andre Braugher), a streetwise black detective with a reputation for being difficult–though no one can be more abrasive than Kojak himself. When Blake is framed for murder, the prosecutor assigned to nail him is Assistant District Attorney Robert Crocker (Kevin Dobson), Kojak's old protégé from his precinct days. Crocker investigates, and discovers the trail leads to his fiancée's father.

Background

Twice CBS tried to revive "Kojak" with exceptionally well made pilots, "The Belarus File" and "The Price of Justice," both of which were based on books and showed there was a great deal of potential left in the series. Along with the "Gunsmoke" revivals, the two "Kojak" movies are the best reunion projects mounted in the last decade. Notably absent from both was Det. Crocker, Kojak's young protégé, played by Kevin Dobson, who was tied up as a regular on "Knots Landing" when they were made.

When a rerun of "The Price of Justice" on May 28, 1989, scored well (15.6/31), it prompted ABC to order new "Kojak" movies as part of its troubled "ABC Mystery Movie" series, of which only "Columbo" seemed to be working. The subsequent "Kojak" movies neither measured up to the original series nor to the two unsold pilots. They were notable for two things: Andre Braugher portrayal of Kojak's new, right-hand man and Kevin Dobson's return as Crocker, now a district attorney, for one movie.

In 2005, USA Network revived/rebooted "Kojak" for a short-lived series starring Ving Rhames.

Telly Savalas in the 1985 television movie "Kojak: The Belarus File."

"Kojak: The Belarus File"

CBS TV movie. Two hours (2/15/85). Production Company: Universal Television. Director: Robert Markowitz. Executive Producer: James

McAdams. Producer: Albert Ruben. Writer: Albert Ruben. Creator: Abby Mann. From a novel by Selwin Raab. Music: Joseph Conlan and Barry DeVorzon.

Cast. Lt. Theo Kojak: Telly Savalas. Peter Barak: Max Von Sydow. Dana Sutton: Suzanne Pleshette. Elissa Barak: Betsy Aidem. Lustig: Alan Rosenberg. Buchardt: Herbert Berghoff. Julius Gay: Charles Brown. Chris Kennert: David Leary. Stavros: George Savalas. Saperstein: Mark B. Russell. Rizzo: Vince Conti. Capt. Frank McNeil: Dan Frazer. Kelly: Clarence Felder. Morgan: Adam Klugman. Mrs. Fitzev: Rita Karin. Rabbi: Harry Davis. Secretary: Margaret Thomson. Bodyguard: Otto Von Wernherr. First Federal Agent: James Handy. Second Federal Agent: Dan Lauria. Assistant D.A.: Martin Shakar. Nicholas Kastenov: Noberto Kerner. Vadim Savatsky: Herman Schwedt. Ristivo: Jose Santana. Lane: Adam Klugman. Sergeant: Michael Longfield. Vladimir Fitzev: Sai La Pera. Film Editor: Brian Keeler. Second Mourner: Lydia Prochnicka.

"Kojak: The Price of Justice"

CBS TV movie. Two hours (2/21/87). Production Company: Universal Television. Director: Alan Metzger. Executive Producer: James McAdams. Producer: Stuart Cohen. Writer: Albert Ruben. From a book by Dorothy Uhnak. Creator: Abby Mann. From a book by Selwin Raab. Music: Patrick Williams.

Cast. Inspector Theo Kojak: Telly Savalas. Kitty Keeler: Kate Nelligan. George Keeler: Pat Hingle. Aubrey Dubose: Jack Thompson. Tim Neary: Brian Murray. Milton Bass: John Bedford-Lloyd. Marsucci: Jeffrey DeMunn. Det. Catalano: Tony DiBenedetto. J.T. Williams. Ron Frazier. Chief Brisco: Stephen Joyce. Danny: Earl Hindman. Quibro: James Rebhorn. Arnold Nadler: Martin Shakar. Lorenzo: Joseph Carberry. Benjamin: Fausto Bara. Mrs. Silverberg: Novella Nelson. Johnson: Kenneth Ryan. Anna: Candace Savalas.

"The Kojak Movies"

ABC series. Two hours, five episodes (11/4/89–4/7/90). Production Company: Universal Television. Executive Producers: William Link, James McAdams. Supervising Producer: Stuart Cohen. Producers: Judith Stevens, Mark Laub, Albert Ruben. Creator: Abby Mann. From a book by Selwin Raab. Music: John Cacavas.

Regular Cast: Inspector Theo Kojak: Telly Savalas. Detective Winston Blake: Andre Braugher. Detective Paco Montana: Kario Salem. Chief George Morris: Charles Cioffi.

The Movies:
"Ariana" (11/2/89)
"Fatal Flaw" (11/30/89)
"Flowers for Matty" (1/4/90)
"It's Always Something" (2/3/90)
"None So Blind" (4/7/90)

"Kojak" (2005)

USA series. 60 minutes. 9 episodes. (3/25/05-5/22/05) Production Company: Universal Television. Traveler's Rest Films. Playa, Inc. Executive Producers: Ving Rhames, Steve Feke, Tom Thayer, Tony Piccirillo. Supervising Producers: Joe Lazarov. Producers: Clara George, Bruce Sandzimier. Music: Mark Snow.

Cast. Inspector Theo Kojak: Ving Rhames. Capt. Frank McNeil: Chazz Palminteri. Det. Bobby Crocker: Michael Kelly. Det. Henry Mussina: Chuck Shamata. Det. Emily Patterson: Sybil Darrow. Medical Examiner: Kelly King.

David Carradine and Keye Luke in "Kung Fu."

Kung Fu
ABC (10/1/72–6/28/75)

Kwai Chang Caine (David Carradine), the soft-spoken half-American, half-Chinese Shaolin priest who fled China after being forced to kill an Imperial

75

Manchu's son who was responsible for the death of his blind mentor Master Po (Keye Luke), became a loner, roaming the West, pursued by Chinese assassins and American bounty hunters. He hated violence, but when he had to, he relied on the deadly art of Kung Fu and other teachings of Master Po.

Over the years, he has become as powerful as his old master, who still appears to him in memories and as an all-knowing ghost. Caine can now levitate, bend iron bars, and perform magical, metaphysical feats, all of which come in handy when the assassins he eluded catch up with him—an evil Manchu lord (Mako), who has trained and hypnotized Caine's illegitimate son Chung Wang (Brandon Lee) to kill his father.

In a show of metaphysical and spiritual prowess, Caine foils opium smugglers who would frame him for another murder, breaks the Manchu lord's hold on his son, and kills his evil nemesis. When all is done, Caine and his son are left alone, master and student, to explore the West and the arts of Shaolin.

In 1987, Caine's descendants still follow his example. Like his ancestor, this Caine (David Darlow) is a gende man who espouses inner peace and lives modestly—he teaches Kung Fu, sells herbs, and helps people in trouble. Perhaps the person who needs his help most is his estranged son Johnny (Brandon Lee), who has become a gang member, served a short jail term for burglary, and hooked up with some dangerous criminals. But thanks to a ghostly visit from the original Caine, Johnny turns away from crime and adopts his father's altruistic lifestyle.

Background

When a continuation of "Kung Fu" failed to excite CBS, Warner Bros, and producer Paul Picard took a new approach, updating "Kung Fu" to the present day for the 1987 unsold pilot "Kung Fu: The Next Generation" (also known at various stages of production as "Way of the Dragon" and "Warriors") which focused on Caine's Chinese-American namesake and descendant, played by David Darlow.

Although the pilot failed to sell, Warner Bros. refused to give up. In early 1993, the studio mounted "Kung Fu: The Legend Continues," a Canadian series produced for first-run syndication. Carradine returned as a modern-day descendent of Caine, and Chris Potter co-starred as his son Peter, a police officer. It lasted until 1997.

David Carradine as Caine a decade later in "Kung Fu: The Movie."

"Kung Fu: The Movie"

CBS TV movie. Two hours (2/1/86). Production Company: Lou-Step Productions, Warner Bros. Television. Director: Richard Lang. Executive Producer: Paul R. Picard. Producers: Skip Ward, David Carradine. Writer: Durrell Royce Crays. From the television series created by Ed Spielman and developed by Herman Miller. Music: Lalo Schifrin.

Cast. Kwai Chang Caine: David Carradine. Sarah Perkins: Kerrie Keane. The Manchu: Mako. Wyatt: William Lucking. Sheriff Mills: Luke Askew. Master Po: Keye Luke. The Old One: Benson Fong. Chung Wang: Brandon Lee. John Martin Perkins: Martin Landau. Old Wife: Ellen Geer. Prosecutor: Robert Harper. Rev. Lawrence Perkins: Paul Rudd. Well Dressed Man: John Alderman. Ching: Michael Paul Chan. Maid: Patience Cleveland. Liu: Roland Harrah III. Federal Marshal: Jim Haynie. Foreman: Roy Jenson.

"Kung Fu: The Next Generation" featured Brandon Lee
and David Darlow as a father and son team.

"Kung Fu: The Next Generation"

CBS pilot. 60 minutes (6/19/87). Production Company: Warner Bros.
Television. Director: Tony Wharmby. Executive Producers: Paul Picard,

Ralph Riskin. Producers: Paul DiMeo, Danny Bilson. Writers: Paul DiMeo, Danny Bilson. From the series "Kung Fu," created by Ed Spielman and developed by Herman Miller. Music: Stanley Clarke.

Cast. Kwai Chang Caine: David Darlow. Johnny Caine. Brandon Lee. Mick: Miguel Ferrer. Lt. Lois Poole: Paula Kelly. Ellen: Marcia Christie. Buckley: Victor Brandt. Carl Levin: Dominic Barto. Cliff: John C. Cooke. Sid: Aaron Heyman. Rob: Eddie Mack. Dave: Michael Walter. Raul: Richard Duran. Security Cop: Michael Gilles. LAPD Officer: Neil Flynn. Student: Mark Everett. Darnell: Oscar Dillon.

"Kung Fu: The Legend Continues"

Syndicated. 60 minutes. 88 episodes. (1/27/93-1/1/97). Production Company: Warner Bros. Television. Executive Producer: Michael Sloan. Supervising Producer: Maurice Hurley. Producers: Gavin Mitchell, Phil Bedard, Larry LaLonde, Susan Murdoch, John Hackett, Bill Taub.

Cast. Kwai Chang Caine: David Carradine. Det. Peter Caine: Chris Potter. Capt. Paul Blaisdell: Robert Lansing. Lo Si: Kim Chan. Capt. Karen Simms: Karen Trotter. Det. Kermit Griffin: Scott Wentworth. Det. Frank Strenlich: William Dunlap. Det. Blake: Robert Nicholson. Det. Jody Powell: Belinda Metz. Det. Mary Skalany: Victoria Snow. Young Peter: Nathaniel Moreau. Sgt. John Broderick: John Bourgeois. Master Khan: Rob Moses. Dr. Elder: David Hewlett.

Tony Dow and Jerry Mathers in "Leave It to Beaver."

Leave It to Beaver
CBS (10/11/57–9/26/58)
ABC (10/3/58–9/12/62)

Theodore "Beaver" Cleaver (Jerry Mathers) should have paid more attention to the sage advice he was getting from his father Ward (Hugh Beaumont).

When we last saw the Beav, he was an adorable, irrepressible kid full of innocence and mischief, who had the most understanding parents imaginable. Perhaps they should have been harder on him because 20 years later, the Beav is a failure as a father and has to go running back to Mayfield, with his kids Oliver and Kip in tow, to live with his perfect mother June (Barbara Billingsley), who is now a widowed city councilwoman.

Not everyone has had Beaver's bad luck. Older brother Wally (Tony Dow) is a successful lawyer and has married his high school sweetheart Mary Ellen, with whom he has a daughter, Kelly. Even Eddie Haskell (Ken Osmond) turned out better; he is the president of Haskell Construction and the proud father of two sons who are the spitting image of their dear dad.

The Beav goes into business with his childhood pal Lumpy and does the best he can at child-raising and, looking to his own father for inspiration, manages to muddle through with surprising success.

Background

Some people just can't take no for an answer. Any hopes of reviving "Leave It to Beaver" should have been crushed in 1983 when CBS, and later the other two networks, rejected Universal's "Still the Beaver" pilot.

But the studio didn't give up. In 1984, it sold the pilot to the fledgling Disney Channel, which produced 26 highly popular half-hour episodes but canceled the series in 1985.

Again, the studio would not accept defeat. With no buyer in sight, Universal went ahead and made 13 new episodes. Rechristened "Wally and the Beaver," and later still "The New Leave It to Beaver," the studio's pet project represented a multi-million dollar gamble that challenged conventional television-business wisdom.

"We believed in it," said Ned Nalle, then Universal's president of pay television. "We had a lot of confidence in the quality of the show. We knew the audience existed. If you put on the Beaver, there is a substantial core audience that will follow the show."

"I think it's unusual that a studio would recognize what we'd done," said Brian Levant, producer and writer of the revival. "When Disney canceled us the studio could have walked away; instead, they decided right there to do what they could to save the family business. I hope and believe we will end up with a syndicatable amount of episodes. That will be the validation of our work. I hope someday we will run side-by-side with the original series and become as ingrained in the public's mind."

Levant got his wish, or at least part of it. Ted Turner's cable network bought the 13 episodes and financed 74 more, ultimately producing a package that was profitable in rerun syndication, where it was still playing at this writing. Whether it can stand up beside "Leave It to Beaver" is yet to be seen.

"This isn't a revival," said Jerry Mathers. "It's basically a new show. We are not redoing 254 episodes of 'Leave It to Beaver.' We want to do a warm, contemporary family show."

"When 'Leave It to Beaver' ended, Wally was going to college and Beaver was going to High School," said Levant. "The concept is that Beaver got his girlfriend pregnant in college, got married, and the marriage fell apart. So he dragged himself home with the kids and found himself. It was easier to let things happen to him than to take control of his life and be the person his parents always expected him to be. By being a single parent with two young sons, he found himself. Now, in the series, we are starting with a single parent who is doing the best he can and relying on his family to help him out."

Mathers had nothing but praise for Levant's approach to continuing the lives of the Cleaver clan.

"If he hadn't come along, we wouldn't have done it. The scripts we were getting were so rotten and outlandish we didn't want anything to do with them," said Mathers. "In one, Beaver is wandering around the country aimlessly after serving in Vietnam. He left his wife and kid. The wife and kid are kidnapped in a bank robbery and Beaver goes in to substitute as a hostage for them. C'mon! That was crazy."

He chalked it up to the studio "having a script lying around and changing the names to make it 'Leave It to Beaver.' It could just as easily have been characters from any other series," he said. "The Beaver character relationships just weren't there. The viewers know the Cleavers very well and wouldn't accept something that didn't understand them as well as they do. In another script, Beaver and Eddie Haskell were best friends. That may be a fine storyline, but that isn't 'Leave It to Beaver.'"

They hope "The New Leave It to Beaver" is, though. "Remember the feeling you walked away with at the end of every 'Leave It to Beaver' show?" asked Levant. "That's what we want."

Tony Dow in "Still The Beaver"

Jerry Mathers in "Still the Beaver"

"Still the Beaver" (The Pilot)

CBS TV movie (3/19/83). Production Company: Bud Austin Productions, Universal Television. Director: Steven Hilliard Stern. Executive Producer:

Bud Austin. Producer: Nick Abdo. Writer: Brian Levant. From a story by Levant and Abdo. Based on characters created by Joe Connelly and Bob Mosher.

Cast. June Cleaver: Barbara Billingsley. Wally Cleaver: Tony Dow. Beaver Cleaver: Jerry Mathers. Eddie Haskell: Ken Osmond. Whitey Whitney: Ed Begley, Jr. Corey Cleaver: Corey Feldman. Mary Ellen Cleaver: Janice Kent. Rusty Stevens: Larry Mondello. Kelly Cleaver: Kaleena Kiff. Oliver Cleaver: John Snee. Kimberly Cleaver: Joanna Gleason. Miss Canfield: Diane Brewster. Eddie Haskell, Jr.: Eric Osmond. Lumpy Rutherford: Frank Bank.

"Still the Beaver" (The Series)

The Disney Channel. 13 episodes (1985). Production Company: Universal Television. Executive Producer: Brian Levant. Producers: Bud Austin, Nick Abdo.

Cast. June Cleaver: Barbara Billingsley. Wally Cleaver: Tony Dow. Beaver Cleaver: Jerry Mathers. Eddie Haskell: Ken Osmond. Mary Ellen Cleaver: Janice Kent. Kelly Cleaver: Kaleena Kiff. Oliver Cleaver: John Snee. Kip Cleaver: Kip Marcus. Gert Haskell: Ellen Maxted. Freddie Haskell: Eric Osmond. Bomber Haskell: Christian Osmond. Lumpy Rutherford: Frank Bank. J.J. Rutherford: Keri Houlihan.

"The New Leave It to Beaver"

WTBS. 77 episodes (9/86–9/89). Production Company: Universal Television. Executive Producer: Brian Levant. Producers: Fred Fox Jr., Peter Ware.

Cast. June Cleaver: Barbara Billingsley. Wally Cleaver: Tony Dow. Beaver Cleaver: Jerry Mathers. Eddie Haskell: Ken Osmond. Mary Ellen Cleaver: Janice Kent. Kelly Cleaver: Kaleena Kiff. Oliver Cleaver: John Snee. Kip Cleaver: Kip Marcus. Gert Haskell: Ellen Maxted. Freddie Haskell: Eric Osmond. Bomber Haskell: Christian Osmond. Lumpy Rutherford: Frank Bank. J.J. Rutherford: Keri Houlihan.

The Life and Times of Grizzly Adams
NBC (2/9/77–7/26/78)

Sometime in the 1850s, Grizzly Adams (Dan Haggerty) fled into the mountains after being framed for a crime he didn't commit—and became a rugged mountaineer with a unique rapport with wild animals. But he risks his freedom to stop his niece from being sent to an orphanage.

"Capture of Grizzly Adams"

NBC TV movie. Two hours (2/21/82). Production Company: Sunn Classic Pictures, Taft International Pictures. Director: Don Kessler. Executive Producer: Charles E. Sellier, Jr. Producer: James L. Conway. Writer: Arthur Heinemann. From the book by Charles E. Sellier, Jr.

Cast. James "Grizzly" Adams: Dan Haggerty. Kate Brady: Kim Darby. Sheriff Hawkins: Noah Beery. Bert Woolman: Keenan Wynn. Liz Hawkins: June Lockhart. Peg Adams: Sydney Penny. Frank Briggs: Chuck Connors. Tom Quigley: G.W. Bailey. Widow Thompkins: Peg Stewart. Daniel Quigley: Spencer Austin. Doc: Jesse Bennett. Ranch Foreman: Shephard Sanders.

The Love Boat
ABC (9/24/77–9/5/86)

On the eve of a Caribbean cruise, Capt. Stubing (Gavin MacLeod) is mourning the death of his wife Emily (Marion Ross), and his daughter Vicki (Jill Whelan), now a travel agent, is doing her best to cheer him up. Isaac (Ted Lange), the new chief purser, is helping a suspended cop nab some fugitive jewel thieves and Dr. Bricker's (Bernie Kopell) new nurse, a former football star named Chris Barnes (John Terlesky) is trying to nab cruise director Kelly (Kimi Johnston Ulrich), who is still hurt from being left at the altar.

Background

Three two-hour "Love Boat" specials aired during the 1986–87 season but the series was effectively dead until CBS aired "The Valentine Cruise" pilot in 1990. It didn't sell. But "The Love Boat" set sail again for UPN in 1998 with an all-new cast headed by Robert Urich as the ship's Captain. In the new show's 16th episode, the cast of the original series reunited for Vicki Stubing's wedding aboard ship. Along the way, Captain Stubing has to choose between running the cruise line and remaining at sea…and Dr. Bricker confesses his love for Julie (Lauren Tewes), the one-time cruise director. Yuck. The series sunk shortly thereafter.

"Love Boat Valentine Cruise"

CBS TV movie. Two hours (2/12/90). Production Company: Aaron Spelling Productions, Douglas S. Cramer Co. Director: Ron Satlof. Executive Producers: Aaron Spelling, Douglas S. Cramer. Producer: Dennis Hammer. Writers: Stephanie Garman, Hollace White, Don Segall, Phil Margo, Barbara Eisenstein, John Harmon Brown. Music: Dennis McCarthy. Theme: Charles Fox.

Cast. Capt. Merrill Stubing: Gavin MacLeod. Dr. Adam Bricker: Bernie Kopell. Isaac Washington: Ted Lange. Vicki Stubing: Jill Whelan. Kelly: Kimi Johnston Ulrich. Paul Royce: Ted Shackelford. Nina Morgan: Shanna Reed. Tony Blanchard: Joe Regalbuto. Maurice Steiger: Rowdy Roddy Piper. Lt. Logan: Tom Bosley.

"The Love Boat: The Next Wave"

UPN Series. 60 minutes. 25 episodes. (4/13/98-5/21/99) Production Company: Spelling Television. Executive Producers: Aaron Spelling, E. Duke Vincent, Ian Praiser. Supervising Producers: Peter Dunne. Developed by: Brenda Hampton, Catherine Lepard *Cast*: Captain Jim Kennedy: Robert Urich. Danny Kennedy: Kyle Howard. Cruise Director Susan Zimmerman: Stacy Travis. Cruise Director Nicole Jordan: Heidi Mark. Chief Purser Will Sanders: Phil Morris.. Security Officer Camille Hunter: Joan Severance. Dr. John Morgan: Corey Parker. Bartender Paolo Kaire: Randy Vasquez

Dennis Weaver in "McCloud."

McCloud
NBC (9/16/70–8/28/77)

McCloud, the country cop on the NYPD, is now a homespun U.S. senator who enlists the aid of his old colleague Broadhurst (Terry Carter), now chief of detectives, and his cantankerous former boss Peter Davis (J.D. Cannon), now police commissioner, to help him bring down the corrupt chemical company that had his niece killed. Along the way, McCloud reunites with his former flame Chris Couglin (Diana Muldaur), now a reporter for the *London Times*.

Background

The charm of the series was completely lost in this reprise, a victim of the baffling decision to scrap the original premise in favor of making McCloud a crime-fighting politician. Shot on location in London and Washington, D.C., the film featured many of the cast members (Patrick MacNee, Simon Williams, David McCallum) who performed in "Return of the Man from UNCLE," a previous effort by writer/producer Michael Sloan.

"The Return of Sam McCloud"

CBS TV movie. Two hours (11/12/89). Production Company: Universal Television, Michael Sloan Productions. Director: Alan J. Levi. Executive Producers: Michael Sloan, Dennis Weaver. Producers: Nigel Watts, Bernadette Joyce. Writer: Michael Sloan. Creator: Herman Miller. Music: Steve Dorff.

Cast. Sam McCloud: Dennis Weaver. Joe Broadhurst: Terry Carter. Peter Davis: J.D. Cannon. Chris Coughlin: Diana Muldaur. Tom Jameson: Patrick MacNee. Also: Kerrie Keane, Roger Rees, Simon Williams, Sonda Currie, Robert Beatty, Michael Cochrane, Melissa Anderson, David McCallum, Patrick Monckton, John Turner, Ricco Ross, Linda Hayden, Mel Cobb, Sion Tudor Owen, Hilary Crane, Ian Taylor, Raymond Marlowe, Alan Polonsky, Adam Richardson, Maxine Howe, Keith Nichols, Paul Stanton.

Make Room for Daddy
ABC (9/29/53–7/17/57)
CBS (10/7/57–9/14/64)

Danny Wilhams (Danny Thomas) and his second wife Kathy (Marjorie Lord) are leading much the same life they led when the kids were still at home. Danny is still a nightclub entertainer, only now Charlie Halper, former owner of the Copa Club, is his agent. Rusty (Rusty Hamer) has joined the Army and married Col. McAdams' (Edward Andrews) daughter Susan (Jana Taylor) and Kathy's daughter Linda (Angela Cartwright) has gone to a Connecticut boarding school.

A year later, Danny and Kathy find themselves thrust into parenthood when Danny's eldest daughter Terry (Sherry Jackson), now married to a serviceman stationed in Japan, leaves her six-year-old son Michael (Michael Hughes) with them for an extended stay while she goes to see her husband. Meanwhile Rusty, out of the Army, goes to medical school.

Background

Shortly after the demise of the long-running "Danny Thomas Show" (aka "Make Room for Daddy"), the cast reappeared in the "Danny Thomas TV Family Reunion," a variety show that contained several skits featuring the Williams family.

The first real attempt to revive the series was on NBC—the one network that had never run the original series, which began on ABC before jumping to CBS. After "Make More Room for Daddy" was rejected, another pilot, "Make Room for Granddaddy," was done for CBS, which also passed. Finally, the revival was pitched at ABC, which bought it, running the continuation for one season before abandoning it.

"Danny Thomas TV Family Reunion"

NBC special. 60 minutes (2/14/65). Director: Alan Handley. Producer: George Schlatter. Writers: Ray Singer, Dick Chevellet, Jack Elinson.

Cast. Danny Williams: Danny Thomas. Kathy Williams: Marjorie Lord. Linda Williams: Angela Cartwright. Rusty Williams: Rusty Hamer. Uncle Tonoose: Han Conreid. Louise: Amanda Randolph.

"Make More Room for Daddy"

NBC pilot. 60 minutes (11/6/67). Director: Sheldon Leonard. Producer: Danny Thomas. Writers: Jack Elinson, Norman Paul. Music: Earle Hagen.

Cast. Danny Williams: Danny Thomas. Kathy Williams: Marjorie Lord. Linda Williams: Angela Cartwright. Rusty Williams: Rusty Hamer. Susan McAdams Williams: Jana Taylor. Charlie Halper: Sid Melton. Louise: Amanda Randolph. Col. McAdams: Edward Andrews.

"Make Room for Granddaddy"

CBS pilot. 60 minutes, (9/14/69). Director: Danny Thomas. Executive Producers: Aaron Spelling, Danny Thomas. Producer: Ronald Jacobs. Writers: Jack Elinson, Norman Paul. Music: Earle Hagen.

Cast. Danny Williams: Danny Thomas. Kathy Williams: Marjorie Lord. Linda Williams: Angela Cartwright. Rusty Williams: Rusty Hamer. Susan McAdams Williams: Jana Taylor. Charlie Halper: Sid Melton. Uncle Tonoose: Hans Conreid. Bunny Halper: Pat Carroll.

"Make Room for Granddaddy"

ABC. 30 minutes, 24 episodes (9/23/70–9/2/72). Producers: Danny Thomas, Richard Crenna.

Cast. Danny Wilhams: Danny Thomas. Kathy Wilhams: Marjorie Lord. Linda Williams: Angela Cartwright. Rusty Williams: Rusty Hamer. Susan McAdams Wilhams: Jana Taylor. Charlie Halper: Sid Melton. Terry Johnson: Sherry Jackson. Michael Johnson: Michael Hughes. Uncle Tonoose: Hans Conreid. Rosey Robbins: Rosey Grier. Bunny Halper: Pat Carroll.

Making the Grade
CBS (4/5/82–5/10/82)

Harry Barnes (James Naughton) is the idealistic dean at Franklin High School in St. Louis, which means he often clashes with the bureaucratic Jack Felspar, the assistant principal. Other faculty members include substitute teacher Jeffrey Kelton (Steve Peterman), gym teacher Gus Bertoya (George Wendt), chemistry teacher Dave Wasserman (Charles MacKenzie), and drama teacher Sara (Alley Mills).

Five years later, Harry Barnes (David Wilson) finds himself teaching history and counseling students at Benjamin Harrison High School, a tough inner city school also known as "The Bronx Zoo." He's still at odds with bureaucratic vice principal Jack Felspar (Nicholas Pryor), but now Harry has a tough, hard-nosed principal more or less on his side—Joe Danzig (Ed Asner). He's also romancing Sara Newhouse (Kathryn Harrold), the English teacher. Other faculty include gym coach/science teacher Gus Butterfield (Mykel T. Williamson), math teacher Matthew Lippman (Jerry Levine), and art and drama teacher Mary Callahan (Kathleen Beller).

Background

Reviving a flop sitcom is nothing new—just look at first-run syndication. But producer Gary David Goldberg gave the practice a new twist.

He took his old half-hour comedy "Making the Grade," which lasted a mere six weeks on CBS in 1982, and reworked it as an hour-long drama called "The Bronx Zoo," which NBC tried all over the schedule. The series failed to find an audience.

"'Family Ties' started as an hour-long drama project at CBS and became a hit as a half-hour comedy at NBC," says Goldberg, creator and executive producer of "Family Ties." "I [hoped] lightning [would] strike twice, but in reverse order."

He felt that "Making the Grade" was "a project that deserved to live that was given short shrift by CBS." If it had been on NBC, he believed, it would have been a hit. But he admits it wasn't all CBS' fault. The show, based on his brother's life, "wasn't done in the proper form originally. The idea needed more weight."

"The hour-long, dramatic form is really more appropriate." Goldberg was too "emotionally committed" to "Family Ties" to devote the energy to developing and producing an hour-long drama, so he hired Patricia Jones and Donald Reiker, the team that produced "Report to Murphy," the flop sitcom that followed "Making the Grade."

He had worked with them on his previous sitcoms, "The Tony Randall Show" and "The Last Resort." More important, the producers had experience writing about high school life—they were, for a time, the executive producers of "Fame," the hour-long drama that became a first-run syndicated hit after NBC axed it in 1983.

The "brilliant" change Goldberg says the producers made with his concept was the addition of the principal as a starring role. The part, which Jones describes as "the Lee Iacocca of schools," was tailored specifically for Ed Asner, who worked with Goldberg on "Lou Grant." Most of the other characters were lifted from "Making the Grade."

The idea, clearly, was to make "The Bronz Zoo" the Hill Street precinct of schools, where faculty members grapple with gangs, drugs, and teenage pregnancy, as well as lack of funding and supplies. And, of course, the intricacy of educational and sexual politics.

91

David Wilson played a history teacher and counselor who was a divorced father raising two kids. Wilson's character was sleeping with the English teacher (Kathryn Harrold), who came from a wealthy family and was constantly frustrated by her students' negative attitude and the school's lack of resources to teach them with. James Naughton and Alley Mills originated the roles in "Making the Grade."

Nicholas Pryor was the by-the-book, narrow-minded vice principal, a part portrayed by Graham Jarvis in the CBS sitcom, and Mykel T. Williamson was a science teacher involuntarily assigned as gym coach by the previous principal. Williamson's character was a reworking of the role played in "Making the Grade" by George Wendt.

The storylines reflected the seamy locale. In the pilot, for instance, the principal fights to retain his in-house day-care center for teenage student mothers. A counselor tries to get a bright gang member to take an upcoming college entrance exam—which the kid misses because he's busted for dealing drugs. And the coach has a hard talk with his students—one of whom boasts about fathering several kids—about birth control.

The pilot underwent some changes before hitting the air. Martin Ferraro, a semi-regular on "Miami Vice," was dropped as the Latin teacher who moonlighted as a travel agent, a role previously played by Zane Lasky in "Making the Grade." Actress Kim Delaney looked too young as the art and drama teacher and was replaced by Kathleen Beller.

At the time, Goldberg was asked whether, if "The Bronx Zoo," like "Making the Grade," had a short life, he would finally give up on the concept. He laughed. "I'll try radio."

"The Bronx Zoo"

NBC series. 60 minutes (3/19/87–6/29/88). Production Company: Ubu Productions, Paramount Television. Executive Producer: Gary David Goldberg. Producers: Patricia Jones, Donald Reiker.

Cast. Joe Danzig: Ed Asner. Jack Felspar: Nicholas Pryor. Sara Newhouse: Kathryn Harrold. Harry Barnes: David Wilson. Mary Caitlin Callahan: Kathleen Beller. Matthew Lippman: Jerry Levine. Gus Butterfield: Mykel T. Williamson. Carol Danzig: Janet Carroll. Roz: Gail Boggs. Roberta: Tyra Ferrell. Virginia Biederman: Betty Karlen. Snyder: Adam Carl. Chris Barnes: Chelsea Field.

Ken Berry, Vicki Lawrence, and Dorothy Lyman (seated) and Allan Kayser and Beverly Archer (standing) in the syndicated "Mama's Family."

Mama's Family
NBC (1/22/83–9/15/84)

Thelma "Mama" Harper (Vicki Lawrence) is a cantankerous woman who is never without a harsh opinion about something–usually about her dimwitted son Vint (Ken Berry), a locksmith who moved in with Mama bringing his two teenage kids, Sonia (Karen Argoud) and Buzz (Eric Brown), when his wife ran off to be a Vegas showgirl. He barely settles in when he marries supermarket checker Naomi Oates (Dorothy Lyman) and she moves in, too. Also living under the same roof is Thelma's sister Fran (Rue McClanahan), a reporter for the local paper. And, of course, every so often pushy daughter Eunice (Carol Burnett) and good-for-nothing husband Ed (Harvey Korman) visit. Another frequent visitor is Mama's other daughter, haughty Ellen (Betty White).

In 1986, Fran has died, Ed and Eunice have moved to Florida, and Vint's children seem to have disappeared, if they ever existed at all. When Ed and Eunice's son Bubba (Allan Kayser) is released from jail, where he has been serving time for car theft, he moves in with Mama.

Background

"Mama's Family" began as a skit on the old "Carol Burnett Show," featuring Vicki Lawrence as cantankerous Thelma Harper, Carol Burnett as her daughter Eunice, and Harvey Korman as Eunice's bumbling husband. (This was strange casting, considering that, in real life, Lawrence is considerably younger than Burnett.)

The family returned in a 1982 CBS television movie entitled "Eunice," which served as a pilot of sorts for the short-lived 1983 NBC series "Mama's Family," which was produced by Joe Hamilton, who also produced "The Carol Burnett Show."

With only 35 episodes of "Mama's Family" completed, the production company, Lorimar-Telepictures, was about 70 episodes shy of the necessary number of episodes to make "Mama's Family" lucrative in syndication, which is where the big money is. So, teaming up with independent stations, Lorimar churned out more episodes—with great success—for a total of 110 episodes, enough to make an attractive rerun package.

Eric Brown and Karen Argoud, Vint's children in the NBC series, were written out of the syndicated revival. Betty White stuck with "Mama's Family," until she defected to join "Golden Girls," co-starring with fellow "Mama's Family" alumna Rue McClanahan.

"Mama's Family"

Syndicated (1986–1990). Production Company: Lorimar-Telepictures, Joe Hamilton Productions. Producers: Joe Hamilton, Rick Hawkins. Creators: Dick Clair, Jenna McMahon.

Cast. Thelma Harper: Vicki Lawrence. Vinton Harper: Ken Berry. Naomi Harper: Dorothy Lyman. Bubba Higgins: Allan Kayser. Iola Bolen: Beverly Archer. Ellen Harper: Betty White.

Robert Vaughn and David McCallum sporting unwieldy weaponry in the original "Man from U.N.C.L.E."

The Man from U.N.C.L.E
NBC (9/22/64–1/15/68)

Napolean Solo (Robert Vaughn) and Ilya Kuryakin (David McCallum) were two suave secret agents working for the supersecret United Network Command for Law and Enforcement, who saved the world from the clutches of THRUSH on a weekly basis for four exciting years. But 15 years later, a lot has changed. Napolean Solo is a womanizing gambler, frittering away the money he has earned with his personal computing business on high-stakes poker. Ilya is fighting hemlines and fashion trends as a clothing designer. At least that is what they are doing when Sir John Raleigh (Patrick MacNee), the new head of U.N.C.L.E., pulls them out of retirement to save the world once again. Seems an old foe has broken out of prison and is threatening the world with stolen nuclear bombs. The men from U.N.C.L.E. are a little rusty, but old skills come back fast.

Background

His features are sharp, hawklike, and his voice has a smooth, measured crispness that underscores his confident demeanor and hints at his capacity for violence. Clad in a black tuxedo, oozing the urbane sophistication that has become his trademark, he eyes his poker hand and considers his options.

And that's when his pen rings.

Startled, he looks up from his hand and faces the curious stares of the men around the table. His pen rings again.

"A new battery in my pacemaker," he says with a smile, excusing himself from the table. He strides to a dark corner, pulls the pen from his pocket, and whispers into it, "Open channel D."

"Ah, Mr. Solo," a voice replies. "I suppose this comes rather out of the blue."

"Yes, my pen hasn't talked to me in some time."

"We have a little job for you...."

The man from U.N.C.L.E. is back in business. His mission: Stop THRUSH from succeeding with its latest evil plot and help CBS bully its rivals into crying "Uncle!" for mercy.

"It's terrifying to get up and suddenly find yourself back in the sixties and then look in the mirror and get back in the eighties. It's a big jump," said David McCallum, who returned with Robert Vaughn to reprise their roles as Ilya Kuryakin and Napoleon Solo in "The Return of the Man from U.N.C.L.E.: The 15 Years Later Affair."

The two-hour television movie was written and produced by Michael Sloan, who would go on to mount revivals of "The Six Million Dollar Man" and "McCloud." Sloan came up with the notion of reviving "Man from U.N.C.L.E." while eating lunch with friends during a break in the filming of his series "B.J. and the Bear."

"I said if they are going to revive something, they ought to revive something fun, like 'The Man from U.N.C.L.E.' And we all said, 'Yeah, that would be great.' It wasn't until some time later that I thought, Why don't I do it?"

It didn't cross his mind again until "B.J. and the Bear" was axed and he began searching for projects for his newly formed production company. Once he decided to do an "U.N.C.L.E." remake, he didn't rush over to MGM to discuss the rights–which would have been the smart thing to do.

"I didn't do it the right way. I went to see McCallum in New York and we had lunch and I asked him if he'd like to play Ilya again. He thought about it and agreed to do it if Robert would do it. So, I went back to L.A., had lunch with Robert, and he said he would do it if David did," Sloan says. "So, I went to NBC and they passed on it because they were trying to get a revival of 'Mission Impossible' off the ground. Then I went to CBS and they liked the idea and they said come back to us with an outline that makes it worthy of a revival."

Robert Vaughn was very happy when he read the script. "This is probably the best script we've ever had for an U.N.C.L.E. show. It's a return to the type of thing we did during our first season–doing James Bond on television. I think we became too silly during the fourth season."

Napoleon Solo and Ilya Kuryakin have long since left U.N.C.L.E. Solo has gone into the computer business while the enigmatic Russian has become a fashion designer of sorts.

"You would imagine that Kuryakin would be in computers and Solo, with his high fashion sense, would be some kind of designer," Sloan says. "So what you do with U.N.C.L.E. is turn that 180 degrees around. That's what makes it U.N.C.L.E."

Neither of the ex-superspies is enjoying his new career. Meanwhile, the head of the now-crippled THRUSH escapes from prison, revives the organization, hijacks powerful nuclear devices from the U.S. military, and holds the world hostage. He wants Solo, the man who put him away, to deliver the ransom personally.

"There's a new U.N.C.L.E. headquarters that's oak paneled as opposed to the stainless steel of the old days," Sloan says. "And you now get to it not through a tailor shop but through a trashy novelty shop on Times Square someplace. We aren't hiding the fact that they are 15 years older. We sort of make a point of it like they did in the *Star Trek II* with Admiral Kirk. They both say,'Are you sure we can still do this?' They're a little older but essentially their characters haven't changed much."

Sloan was always a fan of "U.N.C.L.E." In essence, doing an "U.N.C.L.E." of his own was the fulfillment of a childhood dream. "When I was 19 years old, I had this great idea for a 'Man from U.N.C.L.E.' I had this descendant of Guy Fawkes who was going to blow up the House of Parliament. I wrote 43 pages of it and never did a thing with it. Now all these years later I find myself doing 'Man from U.N.C.L.E.' In fact, there's two lines in this script from that old script."

Sloan and the cast hoped the movie would spark a new series, and they left the door wide open in the final scene.

"They save the world, and they are in this restaurant," he says. "In the Background, as they leave, we hear a radio or TV report that says, 'Air Force One is still missing...' Just as they are going out, their pens ring and their boss says, 'Tell me, are you doing anything for the next few days?' They look at each other and shrug, and we leave it up to the audience to decide: Do they go back to U.N.C.L.E. or not?"

The intrepid **U.N.C.L.E.** pair returns for "**The Fifteen Years Later Affair**."

"The Man from U.N.C.L.E.: The Fifteen Years Later Affair"

CBS TV movie (4/5/83). Production Company: Michael Sloan Prod., Viacom Enterprises. Executive Producer: Michael Sloan. Producer: Nigel Watts. Director: Ray Austin. Writer: Michael Sloan. Based on characters created by Sam H. Rolfe.

Cast. Napolean Solo: Robert Vaughn. Ilya Kuryakin: David McCallum. Sir John Raleigh: Patrick MacNee. Benjamin Kowalski: Tom Mason. Janus: Geoffrey Lewis. Justin Sepheran: Anthony Zerbe. J.B.: George Lazenby. Andrea Markovich: Gayle Hunnicutt. Nigel Pennington Smythe: Simon Williams.

James Brolin and Robert Young in "Marcus Welby. M.D."

Marcus Welby, M.D.
ABC (9/23/69–5/11/76)

Marcus Welby stripped of his stethoscope because he's a doddering old man? Say it isn't so! Who could have imagined such a fate for everyone's most believed general practitioner? When we last saw Dr. Welby in 1976, he was looking forward to many more years in practice with recently married Dr. Steve Kiley (James Brolin). But by 1984, he is a visiting doctor at a hospital where cold-hearted administrators want to nix his accreditation, shoving him aside to make room for young physicians. It takes the efforts of concerned fellow physicians Dr. David Jennings (Darren McGavin) and his son Matt (Morgan Stevens) to get Welby back his accreditation—and prove that advancing age also adds up to a wealth of knowledge and experience. And it isn't long before Welby, black bag in hand, is off to Paris for a speaking engagement and a whirlwind romance, proving old age has nothing to do with being young at heart.

No sooner does he arrive in Paris, haunted by memories of an earlier visit with his late wife Kate, then he travels on to Switzerland, where he meets Tessa Menard (Alexis Smith), a former ballet instructor turned perfume shop owner, who is guardian to her former student Anna Dupuis (Delphine Forest). Anna is a one-time ballet star felled by sudden and permanent blindness (caused by detached retinas) that neither woman seems willing to accept.

They all return to Paris, where Welby befriends them both. He falls in love with Tessa and helps them both accept the permanence of Anna's blindness. He asks Tessa to marry him, and when she spurns him for a married man (Craig Stevens), Welby returns to America and his consultancy at Coast Community Hospital. But Tessa realizes she loves him, and she surprises him at the hospital. The two are ready to begin their new lives together.

Background

"The Return of Marcus Welby" was intended to spin off a new series, "Jennings and Jennings: A Family Practice," in which Robert Young would have been a recurring character. A subsequent revival, "Marcus Welby: A Holiday Affair," focused on Welby's retirement and a late-in-life romance.

Morgan Stevens and Robert Young in "The Return of Marcus Welby."

"The Return of Marcus Welby"

ABC TV movie (5/16/84). Production Company: Marstar Prod., Universal Television. Executive Producer: Martin Starger. Director: Alexander Singer. Producers: Dennis Doty, Michael Braverman, Howard Alston. Writers: John McGreevey, Michael Braverman. Creator: David Victor.

Cast. Marcus Welby: Robert Young. Dr. David Jennings: Darren McGavin. Dr. Matt Jennings: Morgan Stevens. Dr. Hoover Beaumont: Dennis Haysbert. Phaedra Beaumont: Cyndi James Reese. Astrid Carlisle: Jessica Walter. Nurse Consuelo Lopez: Elena Verdugo. Dr. Nina Velasquez: Yvonne Wilder. Pamela Saletta: Joanna Kerns. Perry Mc-Masters: Milt Kogan. Millie Clark: Fran Ryan. Fanny Glickman: Jacqueline Hyde. Angela: Momo Yashima. Blackie: James Carroll. Aaron Glickman: Al Christy. Second Nurse: Lee Armone. First Doctor: Chris Kriesa. Third Nurse: Linda Hoy. Second Doctor: Richard Marion. Fourth Nurse: Cynthia Avila. Second E.R. Nurse: Barbara Mealy.

"Marcus Welby: A Holiday Affair"

NBC TV movie. Two hours (12/19/89). Production Company: Mar-star Productions, Condor Productions. Director: Steven Gethers. Executive Producer: Martin Starger. Producers: Howard Alston, Peter Christian Feuter. Writer: Steven Gethers. Creator: David Victor.

Cast. Marcus Welby: Robert Young. Tessa Menard: Alexis Smith. Anna Dupuis: Delphine Forest. Frank Denton: Craig Stevens. Dr. Wallace: Paul Maxwell. Dr. Price: Robert Hardy. Allen Simpson: Robert MacLeod. Dr. Marcel: Pierre LeClercq. Cece: Pauline Larrieu. French Clerk: Daniel Leger. Housekeeper: Anna Gaylor. Ruth Wilson: Mary Martlew. French Doctor: Alain Klarer. Chef: Douglas Hudgens.

*M*A*S*H*
CBS (9/17/72–9/19/83)

After the Korean War, Dr. Trapper John McIntire ended up on staff at San Francisco Memorial Hospital, where his son J.T. (Timothy Busfield) eventually served his residency. And we know that Col. Potter (Harry Morgan), Father Mulcahy (William Christopher), and Corporal Klinger (Jamie Farr) worked together at a veterans' hospital in Missouri. But nothing was heard from Hawkeye Pierce (Alan Alda), B.J. Hunnicutt (Mike Farrell), Hotlips Houlihan (Loretta Swit), Frank Burns (Larry Linville) or Charles Winchester (David Ogden Stiers).

Walter "Radar" O'Reilly (Walter Burghoff), however, returned to the family farm and married his sweetheart. But when the farm went broke, she left him for another man. Radar moved to Kansas City to live with his cousin Wendell (Ray Buktenica), an unconventional, wisecracking cop, who convinced him to join the police force. So, last we saw of Radar, he was struggling as a rookie officer and trying to win the heart of the girl who ran the local soda fountain (Victoria Jackson).

Background

While "M*A*S*H" was still on the air, CBS mounted a spinoff, "Trapper John M.D.," following the Wayne Rogers character (now played by Pernell Roberts) as he toiled in a San Francisco hospital. The series ran for seven years. But CBS was not so lucky with other attempts to capitalize on the phenomenal success of "M*A*S*H."

Immediately after "M*A*S*H" ended, CBS tried to keep the show alive with "AfterMASH," a continuation featuring the secondary characters–Col. Sherman Potter, Father Mulcahy, and Corporal Max Klinger and his wife Soon-Lee working in a VA hospital. Creatively, the producers never quite figured the show out, and a succession of cast changes didn't help. Despite strong ratings initially, the show's numbers rapidly deteriorated and it was canceled after one season.

Meanwhile, CBS was developing a show around Walter "Radar" O'Reilly (Gary Burghoff). The resulting pilot aired once, without fanfare, and was never seen again.

"Radar" (aka "Walter")

CBS pilot. 30 minutes (7/17/84). Production Company: 20th Century–Fox Television. Director: Bill Bixby. Executive Producers: Michael Zinberg, Bob Schiller, Bob Weiskopf. Writers: Bob Schiller, Bob Weiskopf, Everett Greenbaum.

Cast. Walter "Radar" O'Reilly: Gary Burghoff. Wendell Mikeljohn: Ray Buktenica. Victoria Petersen: Victoria Jackson. Sgt. Sowell: Noble Willingham. Sgt. Bigelow: Lyman Ward. Judith Crane: Sarah Abrell. Elston Krannick: Meeno Peluce. Haskell: Sam Scraber. Bubbles Sincere: Victoria Carroll. Dixie Devoe: June Berry. Singer: Bobby Remsen. Theater Owner: Dick Miller.

Jack Kelly and James Garner in the original "Maverick" series.

Maverick
ABC (9/22/57–7/8/62)

Bret and Bart Maverick (James Garner and Jack Kelly) were two cowardly card sharks traveling the West, just trying to make a buck. The last time we saw them, Bret had wandered off to parts unknown, and Bart was joined by

Beau Maverick (Roger Moore) from England and long-lost brother Brent (Robert Colbert). They seemed destined to perpetrating cons, running scams, and dealing cards until the law, or a bullet, caught up with them first. And, 16 years later, it looks like both have caught up with Bart.

Bret rides into Las Vegas to collect a $1,000 debt from brother Bart. Upon his arrival, he learns that Bart has been killed. Bart, of course, is not dead but in the middle of another of his schemes, one that also involves yet another Maverick relative, Beau's son Ben (Charles Frank), who was educated at Harvard and by some of the toughest poker tables in the land. Ben ends up hitting the trail with con woman Nell (Susan Blanchard), searching together for fun and profit while under the wary eye of Marshall Edge Troy (John Dehner), who distrusts all the Mavericks and frequently encounters them in his travels. Bret, meanwhile, journeys to Sweetwater, Arizona, for a high-stakes poker game.

When he rides into Sweetwater, no one is asking "Who's the tall dark stranger there?" Children run alongside his horse, women gather to gawk, and photographers lie in wait to capture his famous image on film.

"Are you gonna win, Mr. Maverick?" asks a young admirer.

"Well, son," replies Bret with a sly grin, "I didn't come here to lose." And he doesn't. He ends up with $100,000 cash and the deed to the Red Ox Saloon.

With the large booty in his hands, and after "too many trail towns, too few and far between," the legendary gambler decides he has reached the end of his trail to "who knows where." Bret buys a large ranch, settles down to raise bulls, and becomes a partner in the saloon business with the town's ex-sheriff, Tom Guthrie (Ed Bruce).

Yet Maverick seems incapable of truly retiring. The last time we see him, he is on the short end of a swindle, bamboozled by his very own brother Bart.

Background

"Maverick" was more than a legend of the West; it was a legendary television series. Like most legends, it refused to die.

It has been 30 years since "Maverick" premiered, but its influence can still be felt in shows like "Moonlighting," "Simon and Simon," "Magnum P.I." and "Remington Steele."

The Mavericks, Bret (James Garner) and Bart (Jack Kelly), were frontier gamblers who roamed the West in the 1880s and the airwaves on ABC from 1957 to 1962. Maverick was more than just the story of two cowardly card sharks running cons, running from danger, and running from responsibility.

This wry Western, marked by cleverly crafted scripts lampooning the genre, has become both a historic landmark and something of a microcosm of the entire network programming approach from the late 1950s to the early 1980s. Twenty years after the Maverick boys cashed in their chips, all three networks would deal out their own version of a "Maverick" revival.

To understand ABC's pilot "The New Maverick," CBS' short-flight series "Young Maverick," and NBC's "Bret Maverick," one must go back to the original, a Western series which Cecil Smith, the *Los Angeles Times* television critic, then considered "a ring-tailed wonder of a show, the best thing to happen to television since coaxial cable."

Television was a new frontier when "Maverick" premiered, a fact that perhaps was symbolically represented by the astonishing number of westerns on the air. The dozens of lantern-jawed upholders of law and order, differentiated only by the size and style of their weapons, seemed chiseled from the same granite of heroic preconceptions.

Roy Huggins, producer of the hit "Cheyenne," was fed up with the over-kill of altruistic cowboys. So he created the Maverick brothers, gamblers who shunned responsibility but ultimately, and reluctantly, behaved like heroes. "My dream was to do a Western where when the beautiful girl walks up to the hero and says 'Help me, please,' the hero won't say, 'What's wrong?' He'll say, 'The sheriff's office is thataway' and point down the street." The stereo-type-crushing appeal of "Maverick" was almost instantaneous, and the series trounced its competition in the ratings, staying on top for two seasons and making a star out of James Garner.

The episodes that worked best revolved around greed, satirized conventional heroes, and relied on deft characterizations. While every other cowboy series was steadfastly earnest, "Maverick" had a keen comic style built on shrewd writing and casual, self-deprecating humor.

"We nearly killed the cowboy shows altogether," says Garner. "It was hard after watching 'Maverick' to see those guys go around being brave without laughing." At first, Garner was the sole star of the series, but when the producers couldn't shoot the episodes fast enough to meet network demands, a second brother played by Jack Kelly was brought in, along with a second production crew, to relieve some of the pressure.

"I still enjoy a certain diminishing luster for having done 'Maverick,'" says Kelly. "I think we are the only two actors who have been on all three networks playing the same roles." The scripts for the two actors, Huggins says, "were interchangeable," but while the ratings favored both actors, the audiences turned Garner into a star and left Kelly, meanwhile, back at the ranch.

Huggins left the series after two years, taking the ratings with him. Garner stayed on for another year before walking out in 1960 over a contract dispute. Warner Bros. contract player Roger Moore came in as Cousin Beau Maverick, the black sheep of the family, and alternated with Kelly during the fourth season.

Moore left after one year, despite kudos from the Warners top brass and an impressive audience following because "I was not served well, I'm afraid, with the scripts," he says. "They promised that they would tailor them the way I felt they should be. They didn't, so I left. If I had scripts like Roy Huggins and Marion Hargrove used to write, I would have stayed on."

In a last-ditch effort to recapture the James Garner charm, the producers hired Robert Colbert and created a never-mentioned third Maverick brother—Brent Maverick—for him to play. Colbert looked and dressed like Garner, but couldn't garner the same ratings.

"Maverick" halted production, weathered the remainder of the 1961–62 season with reruns from the first season, and then was canceled. If "Maverick" had been just another Western, it would have languished in syndication, just another forgotten show to play off in the wee hours of the night.

In television history, 1979 may become known as the year of the Great Resurrection. "Gilligan's Island," "The Brady Bunch," "Sanford and Son," "Cannon," "The Mod Squad," "The Avengers," "Father Knows Best," and "The Millionaire" were just a few of the series brought back from the dead. Caught up in this knee-jerk nostalgia, ABC assumed television's second generation was ready for a second generation "Maverick."

Charles Frank was introduced as Beau's Harvard-educated son Ben Maverick in "The New Maverick," a two-hour pilot for a proposed series. Garner and Kelly were reunited in guest-starring roles.

"The whole revival trend came because of a lack of creative thinking," says Garner. "I think sometimes it's just easier to go back and say 'let's try this and this' because they are tried and true. The shows may not be right for an era, but I think they think they can go back and win again off some of the old hits."

They did with "The New Maverick," but ABC, perhaps realizing the real attraction was not Frank but Garner and Kelly, passed on the series.

But CBS was interested and ordered a new two-hour pilot entitled "Young Maverick," starring Frank again and his wife, actress Susan Blanchard, as his spunky girlfriend. The pilot led to a six-episode series.

The networks, wary of taking a big financial risk on full 13-episode orders, were falling in love that year with the idea of short-flight series, much to the chagrin of producers who found it impossible to recoup their production costs if they didn't get renewed. It is virtually impossible to syndicate a mere six episodes.

Not many of the short-flights took off. "Hagen," "Beyond Westworld," "Time Express," and "Semi-Tough" were among the many which lived and died in obscurity. "Young Maverick" joined the list.

"I'm not sure the world was ready for a Mom-and-Pop Western," says veteran "Maverick" writer Marion Hargrove, "a Mr. and Mrs. Maverick and all that crap."

Meta Rosenberg, producer of "The New Maverick," believed "Charles Frank just wasn't Maverick." What is Maverick, then? Ask NBC, and they'll say its James Garner.

The nostalgia trend took on a new form in 1981. The straight revivals were replaced by bland imitations. Television stars from years past were dusted off and given new, but strikingly familiar, series. Robert Stack, Gabe Kaplan, Angie Dickinson, Lee Majors, James Arness, Rock Hudson, Mike Connors, and even Fred Flintstone were among the old faces reappearing on screen.

And James Garner, fresh from the success of "The Rockford Files," returned to the role that made him famous in "Bret Maverick," a NBC series which was a perfect example of the rampant practice that season of packaging shows around stars.

"Garner had signed a deal with Warners and NBC to do a series and someone said 'How about Maverick?'" says Gordon Dawson, the creator, writer, and producer of NBC's "Bret Maverick." "That was as deep as it went. It was a safe way for him to go."

Still, Garner says he was "very leery. I didn't want to do it because I don't think you can beat nostalgia. I just wanted a character like Maverick, so they said, 'Why not play him again?'"

The problem was how to bring the character back. "I didn't know whether to do the same old thing or update it," says Garner. "We decided to update it. I couldn't play the same character now and besides, Maverick was 20 years older himself."

So, in the two-hour pilot, Bret wins $100,000 and a saloon in a high-stakes poker game in Sweetwater, Arizona. Maverick convinces the town's ex-sheriff, played by country singer Ed Bruce (who wrote the show's new theme), to run the saloon for him. The gambler buys a ranch, settles down, and tries to hide from his legend.

"We let the action come to him, more or less," says Garner. "It was a little more sedate, I think, because when you get a little older you're not out there shootin' and ridin' and carryin' on with the Indians. The time has gone by. We decided to make him older, like I was."

He may not have wandered the dusty trails to who-knows-where anymore, but locking "Bret Maverick" in the lazy town of Sweetwater every week turned out to be the biggest gamble yet. "We had a lot of trouble with the concept and we were absolutely ready to take the show in a different direction the second year," says Dawson. "Maverick was going to travel more. The last episode pointed the direction we were going."

In the final episode, "The Hildalgo Thing," the ex-sheriff is reelected sheriff, the saloon is occupied by a madame and her girls, and Maverick teams up with a wily young con man played by Jameson Parker, who would later star in "Simon and Simon." Maverick is also working the biggest sting of his career—a $2 million con on a mysterious robber baron. When the industrialist finally appears in Sweetwater, Bret's elaborate con comes to an abrupt halt. The robber baron is none other than Bart Maverick. The last time America sees Bret Maverick, he is laughing and hugging his brother Bart as the original "Maverick" theme swells in the Background.

There was no second season as NBC canceled the series, despite its ranking among the top 30 shows in a season marked by an abundance of flop series.

Three times, in three years, all three networks tried to revive "Maverick"– and failed. Perhaps what eluded them was something Garner realized only recently: "The Westerns had been dead for a long time. We didn't have anything to poke fun at."

Perhaps "Maverick" could still be updated, brought into a contemporary setting. Huggins doesn't think so, unless you count "The Rockford Files," which he co-created with Stephen J. Cannell for James Garner.

"After all, Maverick was a bum and a drifter," he says. "You can't do bums and drifters in a contemporary environment and have the audiences accept them." Bums and drifters? You can almost see Bret Maverick get that pained, put-upon expression on his face. "Bums and drifters sounds a little harsh," he'd say, that broad, beeming smile lighting up beneath those twinkling eyes. "Let's just say we're two self-supporting enterprisers who like to travel."

In the early 1990s, Mel Gibson starred as Bret Maverick in a feature film version of the series. His adversary in the film was an evil Marshal portrayed by James Garner who (spoiler alert!) turned out to be his Old Pappy Maverick…the two of them were running an elaborate con through the entire movie. So the film was something of a sequel of sorts to the TV series…at least nostalgically.

"The New Maverick"

ABC TV movie (9/3/78). Production Company: Warner Bros. Television, Cherokee Productions. Director: Hy Averback. Executive Producer: Meta Rosenberg. Producer: Bob Foster. Writer: Juanita Bartlett. Based on characters created by Roy Huggins.

Cast. Bret Maverick: James Garner. Bart Maverick: Jack Kelly. Ben Maverick: Charles Frank. Nell McGarrahan: Susan Blanchard. Judge Crupper: Eugene Roche. Porker Alice; Susan Sullivan. Homer: Jack Garner. Lambert: Graham Jarvis.

Charles Frank and Susan Blanchard in the short-lived "Young Maverick."

"Young Maverick"

CBS series. 60 minutes, 6 episodes (11/79–1/80). Production Company; Warner Bros. Television, Cherokee Productions. Executive Producer: Robert Van Scoyk. Supervising Producer: Andy White. Producer: Chuck Bowman. Story Editor: Norman Lieb man.

Cast. Ben Maverick: Charles Frank. Nell: Susan Blanchard (Mrs. Charles Frank). Marshall Edge Troy: John Dehner.

Ed Bruce, Darlene Carr, and James Garner in
the third revival, "Bret Maverick."

"Bret Maverick"

NBC series. 60 minutes, 16 episodes (9/81–5/82). Production
Company: Warner Bros. Television, Cherokee Productions. Executive
Producer: Meta Rosenberg. Supervising Producer: Gordon Dawson.
Producers: Charles Floyd Johnson and Geoffrey Fischer. Story Editor:
Lee David Zlotoff. Developed by Gordon Dawson. Main title theme:
Ed Bruce, Patsy Bruce and Glenn Ray, sung by Ed Bruce (with James
Garner in the pilot).

Cast. Bret Maverick: James Garner. Philo Sandeen: Stuart Margolin.
Ex-Sheriff Tom Guthrie: Ed Bruce. Reporter Mary Lou Springer: Darleen
Carr.

Mike Hammer
CBS (1/26/84–1/18/85,
9/27/86–9/9/87)

Mike Hammer (Stacy Keach), is a hard-boiled, smart-ass private eye who attracts women almost as well as he attracts trouble. Hammer works out of New York, often aided by his secretary Velda (Lindsay Bloom) and NYPD Capt. Pat Chambers (Don Stroud). He is constantly at odds with District Attorney Barrington (Kent Williams).

Background

"Mike Hammer" had a very rocky time on television. It took three pilots to sell the series (the first starring Kevin Dobson), and it enjoyed a relatively smooth first season, but its second year was cut short by star Stacy Keach's arrest, and subsequent jailing in England, for cocaine possession. The series was canceled in 1985. When Keach was released from prison in 1986, a new pilot was shot, entitled "The Return of Mike Hammer." It engendered a 1986 continuation of the series (as "The New Mike Hammer"), but the reprieve was short-lived, and Columbia Pictures Television was saddled with not quite enough episodes with which to go into syndication and make back its investment.

In 1989, the studio mounted another "Mike Hammer" pilot but, despite decent ratings, a subsequent series was not ordered and the reruns were sold to basic cable. Nearly a decade later, Keach returned for "Mike Hammer, Private Eye," an incredibly cheap, mercifully short-lived, first-run syndicated series in which the small, beach community of Ventura, California improbably doubled for New York City.

"Mickey Spillane's Mike Hammer: Murder Takes All"

CBS TV movie. Two hours (5/21/89). Director: John Nicolella. Executive Producer: Jay Bernstein. Writer: Robert Edens.

Cast. Mike Hammer: Stacy Keach. Vera: Lindsay Bloom. Capt. Pat Chambers: Don Stroud. Also: Lyle Alzado, Linda Carter, Ed Winter, Michelle Phillips.

"Mike Hammer, Private Eye"

Syndicated. TV Series. 60 minutes. 24 Episodes (9/27/97-6/14/98) Production Company: Franklin/Waterman Productions, Kushner-Locke Company, Jay Bernstein Enterprises. Executive Producer: Jay Bernstein, Stacy Keach, Jeff Franklin, Steve Waterman, Doug McIntyre. Producers: Larry B. Williams, Cary Glieberman, John S. Curran. Music: Eric Allaman.

Cast: Mike Hammer: Stacy Keach. Vera: Shanny Whirry. Deputy Mayor Barry Lawrence: Kent Williams, Capt. Skip Gleason: Peter Jason, Nick Farrell: Shane Conrad. Maya Ricci: Malgosia Tomassi. The Face: Rebekah Chaney

The Millionaire
CBS (1/19/55–9/28/60)

Billionaire John Beresford Tipton still amuses himself by having his executive secretary, Michael Anthony, give million-dollar checks to average people picked at random and then watching how the sudden wealth affects them.

Background
Robert Quarry became the new Michael Anthony in this would-be anthology.

"The New Millionaire"

CBS TV movie. Two hours (12/19/78). Production Company: Don Fedderson Productions. Director: Don Weis. Executive Producer: Don Fedderson. Writer: John McGreevey. Creator: Don Fedderson. Music: Frank DeVol.

Cast. Michael Anthony: Robert Quarry. Arthur Haines: Martin Balsam. Paul Matthews: Edward Albert. Eddie Reardon: Bill Hudson. Harold Reardon: Brett Hudson. Mike Reardon: Mark Hudson. Kate Matthews: Pamela Toll. George Matthews: Ralph Bellamy. Mrs. Matthews: Jane Wyatt. Doreen: Talia Balsam. Judge: Sally Kemp. Maggie Haines: Pat Crowley. George Jelks: Allan Rich. Marshall Wayburn: John Ireland. Clark: Michael Minor. Oscar Pugh: William Demarest. Parker: Milt Kogan.

Mission: Impossible
CBS (9/17/66–9/8/73)

Jim Phelps (Peter Graves) comes out of retirement when his protégé, an IMF team leader, is killed. To bring the bad guys to justice, Phelps assembles a new team remarkably like his old one–Nicholas Black (Thaao Penghlis), former actor and a master of disguise; Grant Collier (Phil Morris), Barney's (Greg Morris) son who graduated MIT at age 16 and is as adept at high-tech gadgets as his father; muscleman Max Harte (Tony Hamilton), who singlehandedly rescued his brother from a POW camp in Vietnam; and beautiful former model Casey Randall (Terry Markwell), who hunted down the terrorists who killed her husband.

But after only a few missions, tragedy strikes. Casey is killed by lethal injection by an evil Third World dictator. She is replaced by Shannon Reed (Jane Badler), a former journalist turned secret agent.

Later, Jim risks his own life to save former IMF agent Lisa Casey (Linda Day George), now a stage producer, from a similar fate when a rogue IMF agent, posing as Phelps, starts assassinating other IMF agents. And when Barney is falsely arrested for murder and sentenced to death by a corrupt foreign government, Jim and his team come to the rescue.

Years later, a retired Cinnamon Carter (Barbara Bain) would be lured back into the fold to find a mole...and would be aided in her efforts by Dr. Mark Sloan (Dick Van Dyke), a crime-solving doctor.

Background

In 1988, a Writers Guild of America strike crippled the industry. The networks, starved for programs, hit on the notion of simply remaking old series, using old scripts, to create something than then–NBC programmer Brandon Tartikoff called "American Originals." Although several series were put into redevelopment (including "Ghost and Mrs. Muir," "The Hardy Boys," and "The Eddie Capra Mysteries"), only two such shows actually made it on the air, both on ABC: six "Police Story" movies (all remakes of old scripts) and "Mission: Impossible," mounted in Australia with Peter Graves and an otherwise all-new cast in all-too-familiar roles. Three old scripts were reshot before the strike ended and new scripts could be commissioned. The production values on the new series were impressive, but the producers would have been better off continuing to dust off the old scripts. The poorly written "Mission: Impossible" limped on for almost two seasons, most of the time deployed in a real-life impossible mission: tackling the "Cosby Show/Different World" juggernaut.

In 1996, a feature film version of the series was released starring Tom Cruise...which, of course, led to a globally successful series of tentpole action movies that had little to do with the original show.

But there was one more, little-known revival featuring one member of the original cast: Barbara Bain returned as Cinnamon Carter for a November 1997 episode of "Diagnosis Murder," the long-running CBS series. In the episode, Carter is brought out of retirement to help solve the murder of a fellow agent and uncover a mole.

Phil Morris, the son of "Mission Impossible" star Greg Morris, also appeared in the episode, though *not* as a relative of IMF team member Barney Collier. Other guest cast included Robert Culp, Robert Vaughn, and Patrick MacNee, though none of them reprised their iconic TV spy roles.

The Cast of the revived "Mission Impossible": Jane Badler, Tony Hamilton, Peter Graves, Phil Morris, and Thaao Penghlis.

"Mission: Impossible"

ABC TV series. 60 minutes, 35 episodes (10/23/88–2/24/90). Production Company: Paramount Television. Executive Producer: Jeffrey Hayes. Producers: Michael Fisher, Walter Brough. Creator: Bruce Geller. Music: Dennis McCarthy. Theme: Lalo Schifrin.

Cast. Jim Phelps: Peter Graves. Max Harte: Tony Hamilton. Grant Collier: Phil Morris. Nicholas Black: Thaao Penghlis. Casey Randall: Terry Markwell. Shannon Reed: Jane Badler. Barney Collier: Greg Morris.

Barbara Bain, Patrick MacNee, Robert Culp, Robert Vaughn, and
Dick Van Dyke in the "Discards" episode of "Diagnosis Murder"

"Discards" (Aired as an episode of "Diagnosis Murder")

CBS. 60 minutes. (11/13/97) Director: Christian Nyby II. Executive
Producers: Lee Goldberg, William Rabkin, Dick Van Dyke, Fred Silverman.
Supervising Producers: David Bennett Carren, J. Larry Carroll. Writers: David
Bennett Carren, J. Larry Carroll. Producers: Barry Steinberg, Jackie Blain.

Cast: Cinnamon Carter: Barbara Bain. Dain Travis: Robert Culp. Alexander
Drake: Robert Vaughn. John Kessler: Phil Morris. Bernard Garrison: Patrick
Macnee. Dr. Mark Sloan: Dick Van Dyke. Lt. Steve Sloan: Barry Van Dyke. Dr.
Jesse Travis: Charlie Schlatter. Dr. Amanda Bently: Victoria Rowell.

Clarence Williams III and Michael Cole in "The Mod Squad."

Mod Squad
ABC (9/24/68–8/23/73)

The sixties are over, and yesterday's hippies are today's authority figures. The Mod Squad has grown up, too, and left police work behind, along with their psychedelic T-shirts, love beads, and leather sandals. But when someone goes gunning for their ex-boss, Deputy Police Commissioner Adam Greer (Tige Andrews), businessman Pete Cochran (Michael Cole), housewife and mother Julie Barnes (Peggy Lipton), and school teacher Line Hayes (Clarence Williams III) reunite to find the hitman.

"Return of the Mod Squad"

ABC TV movie. Two hours (5/18/79). Production Company: Spelling/ Thomas Productions. Director: George McCowan. Executive Producers: Aaron Spelling, Danny Thomas. Producer: Lynn Loring. Writer: Robert Janes. Music: Mark Snow, Shorty Rogers, Earle Hagen.

Cast. Pete Cochran: Michael Cole. Julie Barnes-Bennett: Peggy Lipton. Line Hayes: Clarence Williams III. Deputy Commissioner Greer: Tige Andrews. Commissioner Metcalf: Simon Scott. Dan Bennett: Roy Thinnes. Jason Hayes: Todd Bridges. Buck Prescott: Ross Martin. Johnny Starr: Victor Buono. Richie Webber: Mark Slade. Frank Webber: Tom Bosley. Cook: Tom Ewell. Marty: John Karlen. Kate Kelsey: Jess Walton. Jake: Taylor Lacher. Johnny Sorella: Rafael Campos. Bingo: Byron Stewart. Willie: Hope Holliday.

The Munsters
cbs (9/24/64–9/8/66)

The Munsters, perhaps because they are a supernatural family, haven't changed—or seemingly aged—at all in nearly 20 years. In fact, Eddie the wolfboy is still in high school, and Marilyn is still in college. And the whole family is still adept at inadvertently getting into big trouble. It seems a mad scientist (Sid Caesar) is committing crimes with robots that look just like Herman (Fred Gwynne) and Grandpa (Al Lewis), who find themselves on the most wanted list. They barely manage to get out of that mess when one of Grandpa's experiments goes awry and they're all stuck in suspended animation, emerging in the 1980s to a very different world.

Background
"The Munster's Revenge" was a plodding revival resoundingly trashed by the critics, but it was Shakespeare compared to "The Munsters Today," an

atrociously cheap-looking and laughless sitcom produced by the Arthur Company for first-run syndication.

In 2010, NBC was still on a revival streak, despite disasterous reboots of "Knightrider" and "The Bionic Woman." The network spent two years developing a darker, edgier, bloodier "Munsters" with writer Bryan Fuller, creator of "Pushing Daisies," director Bryan Singer, who'd helmed the X-Men movies and producer Sara Colleton, fresh off of "Dexter." They ended up spending over $10 million on the one-hour pilot and a handful of back-up scripts for the series. What the network ended up with was a pricy, uneven, and very strange pilot that they burned off as a Halloween special. But the network stayed in business with Fuller, giving him a 13-episode commitment for "Hannibal," a series prequel to "Red Dragon" and "Silence of the Lambs."

"The Munsters' Revenge"

NBC TV movie. 90 minutes (2/27/81). Production Company: Universal Television. Director: Don Weis. Executive Producer: Edward Montagne. Producers: Don Nelson, Arthur Alsberg. Writers: Don Nelson, Arthur Alsberg.

Cast. Herman Munster: Fred Gwynne. Lily Munster: Yvonne DeCarlo. Grandpa: Al Lewis. Marilyn Munster: Jo McDonnell. Eddie Munster: K.C. Martel. Dr. Diablo/Emil Hornshymier: Sid Caesar. Phantom of the Opera: Bob Hastings. Igor: Howard Morris. Chief Harry Boyle: Herbert Voland. Detective Glen Boyle: Peter Fox. Commissioner McClusky: Charles Macaulay. Michael: Colby Chester. Ralph: Michael McManus. Pizza man: Joseph Ruskin. Dr. Licklider: Ezra Stone. Shorty: Billy Sands. Officer Leary: Billy Sands. Warren Thurston: Barry Pearl. Prisoner: Al C. White. Slim: Tom Newman. Elvira: Anita Dangler. Mrs. Furnston: Dolores Mann.

The cast of "The Munsters Today."

"The Munsters Today"

Syndicated. 30 minutes, 44 episodes (1988–1990). Production Company: Universal Television, Arthur Company. Executive Producer: Arthur Annecharico. Supervising Producer: Patricia Fass Palmer. Producer: Lloyd Schwartz.

Cast. Herman Munster: John Schuck. Lily Munster: Lee Meriwether. Grandpa Munster: Howard Morton. Marilyn Munster: Hilary Van Dyke. Eddie Munster: Jason Marsden.

"Mockingbird Lane"

NBC. 60 minutes. 10/26/12. Director: Bryan Singer. Executive Producers: Bryan Fuller, Bryan Singer, Sara Colleton. Producers: Jack Clements, Livia Hanich, Loretta ramos, Jason Taylor. Writers: Bryan Fuller, Norm Liebmann, Ed Haas, based on characters created by Allan Burns & Chris Haywood. Music: Jim Dooley.

    Cast: Herman Munster: Jerry O'Connell. Lily Munster: Portia de Rossi. Marilyn Munster: Charity Wakefield. Eddie Munster: Mason Cook. Grandpa Munster: Eddie Izzard. Steve: Cheyenne Jackson. Marie: Beth Grant. Real Estate Agent: Allen C. Liu.

Rachel Dennison, Valerie Curtin, Jean Marsh, and
Rita Moreno in the first "Nine to Five" series.

Nine to Five
ABC (3/25/82–10/27/83)

When we last visited American Household Products in Cleveland, beleaguered secretaries Violet Newstead (Rita Moreno), Doralee Rhoades (Rachel

Dennison) and Judy Burnley (Valerie Curtin) were still at odds with domi-
neering boss Franklin Hart, Jr. (Jeffrey Tambor, Peter Bonerz).

Doralee and Judy have since moved on to Barkley Foods International in
New York, where they join secretary Marsha McMurray (Sally Struthers), a
recent divorcee, in their struggles with the corporate environment.

Background

The series was based on the hit 1980 movie starring Jane Fonda, Lily Tomlin,
and Dolly Parton. Initially, Fonda and her then-partner Bruce Gilbert produced the series. They dropped out and were replaced by James Komack. The
show limped along for just over a season and disappeared until the barter
syndication business boomed. Suddenly, independent stations were hot for
new sitcoms and studios were scrambling for shows to fill the need. Most
studios simply dusted off failed network shows and turned them into a fresh
commodity; 20th Century–Fox was no exception.

"I looked at all the shows we had produced in recent years to find
something to revive," said Michael Lambert, 20th Century-Fox's vice president of domestic syndication. He found 33 episodes of "Nine to Five," and
realized if the company could produce 52 more, it would have just enough
to sell to stations as a daily rerun. By doing so, he said, "I will now be able
to realize some value out of an existing asset that I had and wasn't able to
use before."

"Nine to Five"

Syndicated. 30 minutes, 85 episodes (1986–88). Producers: Lynn Roth,
Michael Kagan, Ava Nelson.

Cast. Marsha McMurray: Sally Struthers. Judy Burnley: Valerie Curtin.
Doralee: Rachel Dennison. Charmin Cunningham: Dorian Lopinto. William
Coleman: Edward Winter. E. Nelson Felb: Fred Applegate. Russ Merman:
Peter Evans. Morgan: Art Evans.

Robert Ginty, James Stephens, and Francine Tacker (seated) and James Keane, Jonathan Segal, Tom Fitzsimmons, and John Houseman (standing) in the original "Paper Chase" series.

The Paper Chase
CBS (9/9/78–7/1/79)

James Hart (James Stephens) was a Midwestern farm boy enduring his first year of law school where he was terrorized by the imposing Professor Kingsfield (John Houseman) and aided in his studies by fellow students Elizabeth Logan (Francine Tacker), Franklin Ford (Tom Fitzsimmons), Willis Bell (James Keane) and Thomas Anderson (Robert Ginty). He also worked part-time at a local pub, run by Ernie (Charles Hallahan). But law school wasn't easy, and some students just didn't cut it. Logan and Anderson dropped out.

As Hart entered his second year, he moved in with Ford and took a job writing for the prestigious *Law Review,* where he worked with icy, uptight, all-business Rita Harriman (Clare Kirkconnell) and the brilliant editor, Gerald Golden (Michael Tucci). He also fell in love with student Connie Lehmann (Jane Kaczmarek), who broke his heart when she decided to study abroad. Bell, meanwhile, became dorm manager and got involved with some of the new first-year students, among them Laura (Andra Millan), who got involved with drugs and, on the eve of her third year, opted to drop out and pursue a career as an artist.

The third year presented new challenges, as Golden graduated and the law review became Hart's responsibility, often putting him at odds with Harriman. Ford's brother Tom entered law school, along with eager new student Rose Samuels (Lainie Kazan), a recently divorced, middle-aged mother.

Hart began to have second thoughts about entering the real world, and found himself romantically drawn to Harriman. Although they slept together, they realized they were better off as friends. Hart was offered a faculty post, and believed he really wanted it—but Kingsfield stepped in and talked the other professors out of giving him the chance, arguing that what was best for the school was not necessarily what was best for Hart, who he felt needed real world experience.

At first, Hart resented Kingsfield, but he came to understand, as usual, the man's wisdom.

Finally, graduation day comes, after three long years that have changed the students' lives. Bell goes to a firm in Boise, Idaho; Ford joins his father's firm; and Hart, whose eloquent graduation speech professes his heartfelt appreciation for Kingsfield, is left to choose between a federal clerkship or a job at a prestigious private firm.

Background

"The Paper Chase" made television history more than once—it was the first series to jump from network to cable, the first dramatic series made for pay television, and the first series produced exclusively for cable by a major studio.

It began as a book by John J. Osborne which in turn became a 1973 movie that earned John Houseman an Academy Award. Houseman reprised his role in the 1978 CBS series, which lasted for just one low-rated, critically acclaimed season.

By all rights, "The Paper Chase" should have been written off as a noble failure and forgotten. But it broke the rules. It stayed on the air. In 1980 PBS reran the 22 episodes and discovered there was a diehard audience of loyal "Paper Chase" fans.

"The show did incredibly well," said Lynn Roth, executive producer of "The Paper Chase" on Showtime. "We tried to interest PBS stations into gathering up enough money to make original episodes. They loved the idea, but they couldn't afford it."

Showtime could. "It didn't take a genius to realize the show had a real loyal following," says Brad Johnson, vice president of current programming for Showtime. "We were looking to develop a quality image for the service and programs that would keep a loyal audience. 'The Paper Chase' fit nicely into that mix."

"The Paper Chase" went into production again four years after its demise and "instead of making the students Peter Pans who lived forever as freshmen, we moved them into their second year," said John Houseman, interviewed during production of the series. "Everyone became a little older, a little more adult, and a little more concerned about the world than they were when they were all terrorized as freshmen."

New characters, including Lainie Kazan as an older divorcee who returns to school, were added, and John J. Osborne wrote several of the scripts.

"I was petrified that people had remembered the show as being so wonderful. What if they remembered something we'd never be able to recreate?" said Roth. "So we took advantage of the freedoms of cable, eliminated the false act ending that commercial breaks make you have and tried our best. We took our time to explore subtleties. We may have made the show a little more intelligent because we were allowed to. We didn't have a network that was constanntly telling us, 'The audiences are not going to understand.'"

"What has always been unique about our show is that it's a serious program about the law, and the teaching of the law," said Houseman. "When we were on CBS, there was a tremendous temptation on the part of the sponsors and everybody to try to jazz the show up. We always fought a rear-guard action to deviate into sex or sentiment."

Those battles were not fought on cable. There were other temptations to worry about. "I think everybody was worried the show would be nothing but nudity and swearing because that seemed to be the appeal of cable," said co-star James Stephens. "But that never happened on 'The Paper Chase.' The writing maintained a very high standard. It doesn't try to ride the crest of a wave and be terribly sensual or adventurous. It's much more true and naturalistic."

Perhaps that is why the show thrived quietly on Showtime for so long.

"I think, and this is going to sound corny, it's because the show is about integrity," said Roth. "I think in this day and age, when you smell something with integrity you want to grab it because it's not in abundance these days. It's a theme that pleases a lot of people on a very deep level."

Houseman attributed the show's appeal to Kingsfield's relationship with the students he horrifies.

"I've always felt that it was simply a recognition on the part of people and students, including high school students, that in everybody's life, there suddenly appears a charismatic teacher who pushes you beyond the limits of what you know is possible of yourself," Houseman said. "We may have hated the teacher, but the teacher made a big difference. The gratitude and acknowledgment of that has a lot to do with the creation of Kingsfield's character."

The decision to end the series was a surprisingly easy one.

"It seemed like the right thing to do," said Stephens. "The characters have matured naturally. I think it's great that the producers decided to take on a final episode rather than let it peter out."

"Some shows are not endless, and it's real sad to see a show become tired. Why not go out with a bang?" says Johnson. "There was a nice, logical way to end the series and maintain the show's dignity."

The show now runs in syndication, and although it's over, the mystique that surrounds it still exists. "It was a prestigious show that always carried this highly regarded reputation," said co-star Clare Kirkconnell. "It was something very rare."

Diana Douglas, James Stephens, John Houseman, Michael Tucci, and Andra Millian (seated) and Penny Johnson, Betty Harford, Peter Nelson, Lainie Kazan, James Keane, and Tom Fitzaimmons (standing) in Showtime's "Paper Chase" revival.

"The Paper Chase" ("Year Two," "Year Three," "The Graduation Year")

Showtime. 60 minutes, 36 episodes (4/15/83–7/15/86). Production Company: 20th Century-Fox Television. Executive Producer: Lynn Roth. Producer: Ernest A. Losso.

Cast. James Hart: James Stephens. Prof. Charles Kingsfield: John Houseman. Franklin Ford: Tom Fitzsimmons. Willis Bell: James Keane. Laura Nottingham: Betty Harford. Connie Lehman: Jane Kaczmarek. Gerald Golden: Michael Tucci. Rita Harriman: Clare Kirkconnell. Laura Kiernan: Andra Millian. Vivian Conway: Penny Johnson. Morrison: Michael Shannon. Zeiss: Worthham Krimmer. Tom Ford: Peter Nelson. Rose Samuels: Lainie Kazan. Prof. Martha Tyler: Diana Douglas.

Raymond Burr on board the U.S.S. *Moray* in "Perry Mason."

Perry Mason
<small>CBS</small> (9/21/57–9/4/66)

Perry Mason (Raymond Burr) has become a bearded appellate court judge and Della Street (Barbara Hale) has become personal secretary to a wealthy businessman (Patrick O'Neal). But when the tycoon is killed, Perry steps

130

down from the bench to defend his old friend, and drafts Paul Drake, Jr. (William Katt), the son of his former investigator, who passed away years go, to handle the legwork. District Attorney Hamilton Burger, Mason's old adversary, has also died, and Julie Scott (Cassie Yates) has taken his place in the prosecutor's office. Mason manages to clear Della and decides to resume his career as a defense attorney, finding a new courtroom adversary in District Attorney Michael Reston (David Ogden Stiers). Della also rejoins Mason, as does Paul, who eventually leaves and is replaced by law student Ken Malansky (William R. Moses).

Background

In 1973, CBS mounted a new version of the Earl Stanley Gardner character entitled "The New Perry Mason" with Monte Markham starring as Mason, Sharon Acker as Della, Albert Stratton as Paul Drake, Dane Clark as Lt. Arthur Tragg, and Harry Guardino as Hamilton Berger. It was a bomb that lasted only 13 episodes. As far as America was concerned, Raymond Burr was the one and only Perry Mason and they weren't ready to accept anyone else in the part. And Burr wasn't ready to come back.

Over a decade later, ex-network chief-turned-producer Fred Silverman, decided to try again…and this time, Burr was up for it (it helped that his last series, "Kingston Confidential" was a bomb and that on his comeback pilot, "Mallory," in which he played another lawyer, wasn't picked up).

The tremendous ratings of "Perry Mason Returns"not only sparked a second wave of TV revivals, but launched a new "Perry Mason" series of television movies which NBC shrewdly, and successfully, used during crucial ratings periods to crush the competition. For instance, the second movie, "The Case of the Notorious Nun" scored an astounding 23.2/42 during the May Sweeps period, and the third, "The Case of the Shooting Star," aired during the November Sweeps period and packed a 23.6/37 wallop. The ratings declined over the years but remained surprisingly potent. The movies might have continued indefinitely if not for Burr's death in 1993.

William Katt, incidentally, is Barbara Hale's real-life son, and guest star Richard Anderson was a regular in the last years of the original series, playing Lt. Steve Drumm. "Perry Mason Returns" was shot on location in Canada. The subsequent films were shot for the most part in Denver, Colorado.

Raymond Burr and Barbara Hale in "Perry Mason Returns," the revival that sparked a successful series of television movies.

"Perry Mason Returns"

NBC TV movie. Two hours (12/1/85). Production Company: Fred Silverman Company, Dean Hargrove Productions, Viacom Entertainment. Director: Ron Saltof. Executive Producers: Fred Silverman, Dean Hargrove.

Producer: Barry Steinberg. Writer: Dean Hargrove. Creator: Earl Stanley Gardner. Music: Dick De Benedictis.

Cast. Perry Mason: Raymond Burr. Della Street: Barbara Hale. Paul Drake, Jr.: William Katt. Arthur Gordon: Patrick O'Neal. Ken Braddock: Richard Anderson. Julie Scott: Cassie Yates. Bobby Lynch: James Kidnie. Paula Gordon: Holland Taylor. David Gordon: David McIlwraith. Laura Gordon: Roberta Weiss. Kathryn Gordon: Kerrie Keane. Lt. Cooper: Al Freeman, Jr. Sgt. Stratton: Paul Hubbard. Chris: Lindsay Merrihew. Lianne: Kathy Lasky. Judge Norman Whitewood: Charles Macaulay. D.A. Jack Welles: Cec Linder. Mrs. Jeffreis: Carolyn Hetherington. Dr. Henderson: David Bolt. Gas Station Attendant: John MacKenzie. Mr. Williams: Frank Adamson. Vinnie: Doug Lennox. Frank Lynch: Ken Pogue. Mrs. Lynch: Doris Petrie. Salesgirl: Mag Huffman.

"The Perry Mason Movies"

NBC TV movie series (1986–1993). Production Company: Fred Silverman Company, Dean Hargrove Productions Viacom Entertainment. Executive Producers: Fred Silverman, Dean Hargrove, Joel Steiger. Producers: Peter Katz, David Soloman, Billy Ray Smith. Creator: Earl Stanley Gardner. Music: Dick De Benedictis. Theme: Fred Steiner.

"Case of the Notorious Nun" (5/25/86)
"Case of the Shooting Star" (11/9/86)
"Case of the Lost Love" (2/23/87)
"Case of the Sinster Spirit" (5/24/87)
"Case of the Murdered Madam" (10/4/87)
"Case of the Scandalous Scoundrel" (11/15/87)
"Case of the Avenging Ace" (2/28/88)
"Case of the Lady in the Lake" (5/15/88)
"Case of the Lethal Lesson" (2/12/89)
"Case of the Musical Murder" (4/9/89)
"Case of the All-Star Assassin" (11/19/89)

"Case of the Poisoned Pen" (1/21/90)
"Case of the Desperate Deception" (3/11/90)
"Case of the Silenced Singer" (5/20/90)
"Case of the Defiant Daughter" (9/30/90)
"Case of the Ruthless Reporter" (1/6/91)
"Case of the Maligned Mobster" (2/11/91)
"Case of the Glass Coffin" (5/13/91)
"Case of the Fatal Fashion (9/24/91)
"Case of the Fatal Framing" (3/1/92)
"Case of the Reckless Romeo" (5/5/92)
"Case of the Heart-broken Bride" (10/30/92)
"Case of the Skin-Deep Scandal" (2/19/93)
"Case of the Telltale Talk Show Host (5/21/93)
"Case of the Killer Kiss" (11/19/93)

Peter Gunn
NBC (9/22/58–9/26/60)
ABC (10/3/60–9/25/61)

Peter Gunn (Craig Stevens) is an urbane, debonair detective with a love for jazz and an even greater love for Edie (Lola Albright), who sings at his favorite hang-out, Mother's—run, of course, by Mother (Hope Emerson, Minerva Urecal). His friend on the force is weary Lt. Jakoby (Herschel Bernardi).

Background

Craig Stevens reprised his role in Blake Edward's 1967 theatrical revival *Gunn*, while Ed Asner played Lt. Jakoby and Laura Devon portrayed Edie. Herschel Bernardi was unable to reprise his role as he was contractually bound to a Broadway show. An unsatisfactory follow-up, the film is notable as one of the first films to display Blake Edwards' ongoing fascination with sexual role reversals, a theme he would return to often (*Pink Panther Strikes Again*, *Victor/Victoria*, *Switch*, etc.).

In 1989, Edwards tackled "Peter Gunn" again, this time with a new cast, for New World Television, where he also intended to do a new version of "The Rogues."

At the time, several studios were vying for the chance to operate ABC's envisioned "Mystery Wheel" franchise–a weekly, alternating series of television movies–and "Peter Gunn" and George Segal's "Murphy's Law" were both designed as "spokes" by New World Television. Ultimately, the network passed on "Peter Gunn" and bought "Murphy's Law" as a series, ostensibly to lead in to the wheel, which it gave to Universal (*see* "Columbo" and "Kojak" for more), which had produced both the "Wednesday Mystery Movie" and the "Sunday Mystery Movie" for NBC years earlier. The latter featured such hits as "McMillan and Wife," "McCloud," "Columbo," and "Banacek."

Craig Stevens will always be Peter Gunn, but Peter Strauss did an admirable job all the same, capturing the urbane charm of the detective hero. The unsold pilot also featured one of the best fight scenes ever staged on television.

Gunn

Theatrical. 90 minutes (1967). Director: Blake Edwards. Producer: Tony Adams. Writers: Blake Edwards, William Peter Blatty. Music: Henry Mancini.

Cast. Peter Gunn: Craig Stevens. Lt. Jakoby: Edward Asner. Edie: Laura Devon. Also: Helen Traubel, Sherry Jackson, Albert Paulsen.

"Peter Gunn" (aka "Rogue Cops")

ABC TV movie. Two hours (4/23/89). Production Company: The Blake Edwards Co., New World Television. Director: Blake Edwards. Executive Producers: Blake Edwards, Tony Adams. Writer: Blake Edwards. Music: Henry Mancini.

Cast. Peter Gunn: Peter Strauss. Lt. Jacoby: Peter Jurasik. Edie: Barbara Williams. Maggie: Jennifer Edwards. Tony Amatti: Charles Cioffi. Spiros: Richard Portnow. Sheila: Debra Sandlund. Mother: Pearl Bailey. Speck: David Rappaport.

Peyton Place
ABC (9/15/64–6/2/69)

In 1977, tragedy strikes Peyton Place when Rodney Harrington (Ryan O'Neal) and Alison MacKenzie (Mia Farrow) are murdered by an outcast returning for revenge.

Collective amnesia, or a time warp, seems to have struck Peyton Place by the time 1985 rolls around. Alison Mackenzie isn't dead, she's just missing-and has been for 20 years, ever since she left Rodney at the altar. Now, her long-lost daughter comes to town.

Background

Four members of the original cast (Nelson, Connelly, Jillson, Malone) showed up for the first reunion. The size doubled for the second with the addition of Parkins, Morrow, Warrick, and Douglas. "Peyton Place: The Next Generation" simply picked up where the old series left off, ignoring events in the previous "Murder in Peyton Place," which also picked up where the old series left off. At the time of this writing, yet another "Peyton Place" revival was in the works.

"Murder in Peyton Place"

NBC TV movie. Two hours (10/3/77). Production Company: Peter Katz Productions, 20th Century-Fox Television. Director: Bruce Kessler. Executive Producer: Paul Monash. Producer: Peter Katz. Writer: Richard DeRoy. From characters created by Grace Metalious. Music: Laurence Rosenthal. Theme: Franz Waxman.

Cast. Norman Harrington: Christopher Connelly. Dr. Michael Rossi: Ed Nelson. Elliot Carson: Tim O'Connor. Jill Harrington: Joyce Jillson. Constance MacKenzie Carson: Dorothy Malone. Stella Chernak: Stella Stevens. Ellen Considine: Marj Dusay. Denise Haley: Charlotte Stewart. Springer: Kaz Garas. Tommy Crimpton: James Booth. Bonnie Buehler: Kimberly Beck. Betty: Janet Margolin. Steven Cord: David Hedison. Carla Cord: Linda Gray. Linda: Catherine Bach. Billie Kaiserman: David Kyle. Stan: Jonathan

Goldsmith. Jay Kamens: Norman Burton. Kaiserman: Charles Siebert. Andy Considine: Chris Nelson. Tristan: Robert Deman. Ruth: Gale Sladstone. David Roerich: Edward Bell.

"Peyton Place: The Next Generation"

NBC TV movie. Two hours (5/13/85). Production Company: Michael Filerman Productions, 20th Century-Fox Television. Director: Larry Elikann. Executive Producer: Michael Filerman. Producer: Terry Morse, Jr. Writer: Rita Lakin. From characters created by Grace Metalious. Music: Jerrold Immel. Theme: Franz Waxman.

Cast. Dr. Michael Rossi: Ed Nelson. Constance MacKenzie Carson: Dorothy Malone. Elliot Carson: Tim O'Connor. Norman Harrington: Christopher Connelly. Betty Anderson: Barbara Parkins. Rita Jacks Harrington: Pat Morrow. Ada Jacks: Evelyn Scott. Hannah Cord: Ruth Warwick. Steven Cord: James Douglas. Kelly Carson: Deborah Goodrich. Dana Harrington: Bruce Greenwood. Megan MacKenzie: Marguerite Hickey. Joey Harrington: Tony Quinn. Dorian Blake: John Beck. Dr. Christopher: Randy Moore. Chuck Daly: Scott Everhart.

Police Squad
ABC (3/4/82–3/25/82)

Lt. Frank Drebin (Leslie Nielsen) is a detective working out of Police Squad, an elite unit of the police force. His boss is Capt. Ed Hocken (Alan North, George Kennedy). His lab man is Ted Olsen (Ed Williams). He gets help from Det. Nordberg (Peter Lupus, O.J. Simpson), and the word on the street from shoeshiner Johnny (William Duell).

His biggest assignment comes when he stumbles—literally—on a plot by an evil tycoon (Ricardo Montalban) to kill visiting Queen Elizabeth. Drebin foils the plot and falls in love with the tycoon's assistant Jane Spencer (Priscilla Presley).

Later, Drebin is working out of Washington, D.C. He and Jane have split up. She's working for Dr. Meinheimer, who is kidnapped by an evil oil tycoon

(Robert Goulet) and replaced by an evil double intent on derailing government energy policies that favor alternatives to oil, coal, and nuclear power. Drebin saves the world and wins the girl.

Background

"Police Squad" was a frequently hilarious spoof of the Quinn Martin/Jack Webb brand of television cop shows, brilliantly satirizing the dramatic and stylistic conventions of the genre. And casting Leslie Nielsen was a master stroke; beyond the innate comic sensibility he revealed in the Zucker Brothers' previous effort, *Airplane*, his face was strongly associated in the American psyche with cop shows, since he had guest-starred in nearly every one of them made in the last 25 years.

Although "Police Squad" lasted a mere six episodes, it developed something of a cult following. When it was released on home video, its tremendous popularity inspired Paramount to do something that it had done once before—revive a failed series with a cult following as a big-budget feature.

They were rewarded for the risk. *The Naked Gun* filled a void left by the death of Peter Sellers, and with him Inspector Clouseau. The first film and its sequels were box office sensations.

Attempting to capitalize on the success, CBS tried rerunning the "Police Squad" episodes during the summer of 1991, but surprisingly few people bothered to watch. Perhaps they owned the video.

The Naked Gun: From the Files of Police Squad

Paramount Pictures. Theatrical. (1988). Director: David Zucker. Producer: Robert K. Weiss. Writers: Jerry Zucker, Jim Abrahams, David Zucker, Pat Proft.

Cast. Frank Drebin: Leslie Nielsen. Ed Hocken: George Kennedy. Jane Spencer: Priscilla Presley. Nordberg: O.J. Simpson. Vincent Ludwig: Ricardo Montalban. Dr. Ted Olsen: Ed Williams. Mayor: Nancy Marchand. Mrs. Nordberg: Susan Beaubion. Queen Elizabeth: Jeannette Charles. Al: Tiny

Ron. Stephie: Winifred Freedman. Pahpshmir: Raye Birk. Enrico Pallazzo: Tony Brafa. Foreman: Joe Grifasi.

The Naked Gun 2 ½: The Smell of Fear

Paramount Pictures. Theatrical. (1991). Production Company: Zucker/ Abrahams/Zucker. Director: David Zucker. Executive Producers: Jerry Zucker, Jim Abrahams, Gil Netter. Producer: Robert K. Weiss. Writers: David Zucker, Pat Proft.

Cast. Frank Drebin: Leslie Nielsen. Ed Hocken: George Kennedy. Jane Spencer: Priscilla Presley. Nordberg: O.J. Simpson. Quentin Hapsburg: Robert Goulet. Dr. Ted Olsen: Ed Williams. Baggett: Lloyd Bochner. Dr. Meinheimer/Earl Hacker: Richard Griffiths. Dunwell: Peter Mark Richman. Fenzwick: Tim O'Connor. Commissioner Brumford: Jacqueline Brooks. Hector Savage: Anthony James. George Bush: John Roarke. Barbara Bush: Margery Ross. John Sununu: Peter Van Norden. Winnie Mandela: Gail Neely.

The Naked Gun 33 1/3: The Final Insult

Paramount Pictures. Theatrical (1994) Production Company: Zucker/ Abrahams/Zucker. Director: Peter Segal. Executive Producers: Jerry Zucker, Jim Abrahams, Gil Netter. Producer: Robert K. Weiss, Robert LoCash. Writers: David Zucker, Pat Proft, Robert LoCash, based on characters created by Jim Abrahams, David Zucker, and Jerry Zucker. Music: Ira Newborn.

Cast. Frank Drebin: Leslie Nielsen. Ed Hocken: George Kennedy. Jane Spencer: Priscilla Presley. Nordberg: O.J. Simpson. Rocco: Fred Ward. Muriel: Kathleen Freeman. Tanya: Anna Nicole Smith. Louise: Ellen Greene. Clayton: Matt Roe. Dr. Eisendrath: Earl Boen. Bobbi: Rosalind Allen. Big Hairy Con: Randall 'Tex' Cobb. Dominatrix: Julie Strain. Conductor: Bill Erwin. Boy of Geriatric Park: Taran Killam. Girl of Geriatric Park: Marianne Davis. Also, Ann B. Davis, Weird Al Yankovich, Mary Lou Retton, Vanna White, Pia Zadora, Florence Henderson, as herself.

Route 66
cbs (10/7/60–9/18/64)

Tod Stiles (Martin Milner) was left penniless when his wealthy father died. He teamed up with Buzz Murdock (George Maharis), a streetwise New Yorker who was one of his father's employees. They bought a 1960 Corvette and hit the road in search of adventure. Buzz eventually left Tod to wander on his own, and Tod teamed up with a Vietnam vet named Lincoln Case (Glenn Corbett). Tod eventually got married to a woman named Mona (Barbara Eden) and gave up the open road.

Buzz finds out years later that a weekend affair with Molly Lewis, a truck-stop waitress in Gainesville, made him a father. He doesn't rush back into her arms, nor does he send checks. But 20 years later, when Buzz dies, he wills everything he owns to Nick Lewis, the son he never met. The only thing Buzz owns is that 1960 Corvette. Seems Nick doesn't have much direction in his life, and finding that Corvette gives him one-sort of. Nick takes the Corvette on the road to find himself. Along the way, he picks up a smooth-talking hitchhiker named Arthur Clark, a conniving cad who has been thrown out by his family. They quickly become friends and take on the open road together.

Background

The revival began with an unsold, and never-aired pilot that starred Brent David Fraser and Andrew Lowery. The show was recast with Dan Cortese and James Wilder and lasted for a mere four episodes. The reviews were not kind. Tom Shales said the pilot went from "merely tolerable to intensely irritating," while Variety noted "the current incarnation seems instantly dated and unintentionally nostalgic…while writer/co-exec producer Peyton tries to inject a contemporary feel with the pseudo-hip dialogue for Clark, his efforts mostly fall flat."

"Route 66" (Unaired Pilot)

NBC pilot. 60 minutes (1992). Production Company: Columbia Pictures Television, Herbert B. Leonard Productions, Propaganda Films. Executive Producers: Herbert B. Leonard, Harley Peyton. Writer: Harley Peyton. Creator: Stirling Silliphant. *Cast:* Brent David Fraser. Andrew Lowery.

"Route 66"

NBC series. 60 minutes. Four episodes (6/8/93). Production Company: Columbia Pictures Television, Herbert B. Leonard Productions, Propaganda Films, Fabulous Lost Cities. Executive Producers: Herbert B. Leonard, Harley Peyton. Producer: Steve Beers. Creator: Stirling Silliphant. Music: Warren Zevon. *Cast:* Arthur Clark: Dan Cortese. Nick Lewis: James Wilder.

Redd Foxx in "Sanford and Son."

Sanford and Son
NBC (1/14/72–9/2/77)

Cantankerous Fred Sanford (Redd Foxx) is still running his Los Angeles junkyard, but since his son Lamont (Demond Wilson) is working on the

Alaska pipeline, he's taken in a heavy-set white partner, Cal Petty (Dennis Burkley), who lives with him. But this is a small adjustment to make compared to the fireworks his romance with rich Beverly Hills widow Evelyn Lewis (Marguerite Ray) is causing with her daughter Cissy (Suzanne Stone) and her stuffy butler Winston (Percy Rodriquez).

"Sanford"

NBC TV series. 30 minutes, 23 episodes (3/15/80–7/10/81). Director: Jim Drake. Executive Producer: Mort Lachman. Producers: Sy Rosen, Larry Rhine, Mel Tolkin. Music: Quincy Jones.

Cast. Fred Sanford: Redd Foxx. Cal Petty: Dennis Burkley. Evelyn Lewis: Marguerite Ray. Cissy Lewis: Suzanne Stone. Winston: Percy Rodrigues. Clara: Cathy Cooper. Aunt Esther: LaWanda Page. Cliff Anderson: Clinton Derricks-Carroll. Officer Smitty: Hal Williams. Officer Hoppy: Howard Platt. Grady Wilson: Whitman Mayo. Rollo: Nathaniel Taylor.

Sea Hunt
syndicated (1957–61)

These are the adventures of Mike Nelson (Ron Ely), a former Navy frogman who goes freelance and who, we discover, has a daughter Jennifer (Kimberly Sissons) who is a marine biologist and sometimes helps out her dad.

Background
Initially MGM/UA Television planned to revive both "Sea Hunt" and "Rat Patrol," the 1966–68 ABC military yarn with Christopher George, as half-hour, first-run dramas for fall 1987. While stations were willing to accept the new "Sea Hunt," they rejected "Rat Patrol," which was slated to star Robert Forster.

The two series were MGM/UA's way of saying "we want to be in first-run in a meaningful way," said Dick Cignarelli, then MGM/UA's executive vice president of domestic syndication. "Both shows had enormous popularity in their original runs." But the two series were revivals in name only, featuring none of the original cast members or production staff of the old shows.

Ron Ely, of television "Tarzan" fame, took over for Lloyd Bridges in the new "Sea Hunt" as the ex-Navy frogman turned deep-sea adventurer. Melissa Sue Anderson, best known for her years on "Little House on the Prairie," was initially cast as his daughter and Brandon Douglas as his son "to add family appeal," said George Paris, then MGM/UA's vice president of first-run development. Anderson bowed out before production and was replaced by Kimberly Sissons. Leonard Kaufman, whose credits include "Hawaii 5–0," was set to produce the series.

"We've got proven titles, formats that work, and based on the receptivity to the shows in the past, we feel the new shows will be greeted with the same receptivity in the future," predicted Paris. But is it really "Sea Hunt" if it's missing the creative elements that were integral parts of the shows before? "That's saying 'Sea Hunt' was Lloyd Bridges and that's putting less emphasis on the concepts," Paris said. "We are placing the emphasis on the concepts—concepts which worked—rather than on the actors who played the roles."

"Sea Hunt" was budgeted at $350,000–400,000 and was sold on the basis of a presentation film. The studio opted to go with remakes rather than create original programming because "we have to go with what we think we can sell," said Paris. "The receptivity in the marketplace tends to be for those shows that have had a previous successful history."

"Sea Hunt"

Syndicated. MGM/UA Television. 30 minutes, 13 episodes (1987). Production Company: MGM/UA Television. Producer: Leonard Kaufman.

Cast. Mike Nelson: Ron Ely. Jennifer Nelson: Kimberly Sissons.

Running in slow motion: Lindsay Wagner in "The Bionic Woman" and Lee Majors in "The Six Million Dollar Man"

Six Million Dollar Man
ABC (10/20/73–3/6/78)

The Bionic Woman
ABC (1/14/76–5/4/77)
NBC (9/10/77–9/2/78)

Steve Austin and Jaime Sommers, estranged bionic lovers and former spies, have retired from the Office of Strategic Information, which is still being run by Oscar Goldman (Richard Anderson). Steve has become a charter boat captain while Jaime has become a psychological counselor helping disturbed teens. (Who knows what has happened to her bionic dog, Max.) They are brought back into action by Oscar Goldman to battle a maniacal villain (Martin Landau). In the midst of it all, they relive (via flashbacks) and rekindle their ill-fated romance. But tragedy strikes when Steve's never-before-mentioned estranged son Michael (Tom Schanley), an Air Force test pilot, is nearly killed in a crash and, like his father, is fitted with bionic parts (including a laser-firing eye) to make up for his lost limbs and organs. Jaime uses her psychological skills to help soothe Michael's feelings of freakishness, and he defeats the bad guys, reconciles with his father, and even joins OSI. Steve and Jaime, meanwhile, look forward to exploring their reborn romance.

When a bionic bad guy infiltrates OSI and steals important papers, suspicion falls on Steve and Jaime. Meanwhile, Oscar's wisecracking nephew Jim (Jeff Yagher) is in love with Kate Mason (Sandra Bullock), a woman who has been wheelchair bound since she was six due to a degenerative muscle disease. Now she has been fitted with newly designed bionic parts—nuclear capillaries and a computerized brain—that make her the ultimate agent. Together, she and Jim infiltrate the World Unity Games to unmask the double agent. Once the evil plot has been foiled, Steve Austin attempts a superfeat even his bionic parts cannot prepare him for—he asks Jaime to marry him. She accepts, of course.

Background

The first revival represented an attempt to mount a spinoff of "The Six Million Dollar Man" and "The Bionic Woman" based on the adventures of Steve Austin's never-before-mentioned son (Tom Schanley). When that approach failed, NBC tried again, this time with a woman, played by Sandra Bullock. And when that failed, it seemed like it was over for the bionic duo. But five years later, CBS commissioned a one-off movie, "Bionic Ever After," that finally brought Steve and Jaime to the alter.

Michael Sloan, the man responsible for these revivals, is the undisputed revival king. His credits include "Return of the Man from U.N.C.L.E.," "Return of Sam McCloud," and USA's resurrected "Alfred Hitchcock Presents," and 1993's "Kung Fu: The Legend Continues."

In 2007, inspired by the success of the rebooted "Battlestar Galactica" on the Syfy Channel, NBC decided to reboot "The Bionic Woman." They brought in "Battlestar Galatica" producer David Eick and cast member Katie Sackhoff in a recurring role as an "evil" Bionic Woman. But salting the all-new, "grittier" show with moonlighting Galactica talent didn't help. The re-imagined "The Bionic Woman" was widely panned, bedeviled by constant creative turmoil that led to multiple producers leaving the show, and was canceled after only eight, awful episodes.

Steve Austin (Lee Majors) and Jaime Sommers (Lindsay
Wagner), together at last, in "The Return of the Six
Million Dollar Man and the Bionic Woman."

"The Return of the Six Million Dollar Man and the Bionic Woman"

NBC TV movie. Two hours (5/17/87). Production Company: Michael Sloan
Productions, Universal Television. Director: Ray Austin. Executive Producer:
Michael Sloan. Producer: Bruce Lansbury. Writer: Michael Sloan. From a story
by Michael Sloan and Bruce Lansbury. From the book *Cyborg* by Martin Caidin.

Cast. Steve Austin: Lee Majors. Jaime Sommers: Lindsay Wagner. Oscar
Goldman: Richard Anderson. Michael Austin: Tom Schanley. Dr. Rudy
Wells: Martin E. Brooks. Charles Stenning: Martin Landau. Jim Castillian:
Lee Majors II. John Praiser: Gary Lockwood. Sally: Deborah White. Kyle:
Robert Hoy. Duke Rennecker: Patrick Pankhurst. Santiago: Terry Kiser.

"The Bionic Showdown"

NBC TV movie. Two hours (4/30/89). Production Company: Universal Television. Director: Alan Levi. Executive Producer: Michael Sloan. Producers: Nigel Watts, Bernie Joyce. Co-Producers: Lee Majors, Richard Anderson. Writers: Michael Sloan, Brock Choy. From a story by Michael Sloan and Robert De Laurentis.

Cast. Steve Austin: Lee Majors. Jaime Sommers: Lindsay Wagner. Oscar Goldman: Richard Anderson. Dr. Rudy Wells: Martin E. Brooks. Kate Mason: Sandra Bullock. Jim Goldman: Jeff Yagher. Castillian: Lee Majors II. Gen. McAllister: Robert Lansing. Esterman: Josef Sommer. Devlin: Geraint Wyn Davies.

"Bionic Ever After"

CBS TV Movie. Two Hours. (11/29/94) Production Company: Universal Television. Director: Steve Stafford. Executive Producers: Richard Anderson, Michael O. Gallant, Michael Sloan. Writers: Michael Sloan, Norman Morrill, based on the novel "Cyborg" by Martin Caidin. Music: Ron Ramin.

Cast. Steve Austin: Lee Majors. Jaime Sommers: Lindsay Wagner. Oscar Goldman: Richard Anderson. Dr. Rudy Wells: Martin E. Brooks. Kimberly Haviland: Farrah Forke. Carolyn MacNamara: Anne Lockhart. John MacNamara: Alan Sadler. Miles Kendrick: Geordie Johnson. Astaad Rashid: Ivan Sergei. Jim Castillian: Lee Majors II. Also, Dave Thomas as himself.

"The Bionic Woman"

NBC Series. 60 Minutes. 8 episodes (9/26/2007-11/28/2007). Production Company: Universal Television. Executive Producers: David Eick, Laeta Kalogridis, Jason Smilovic, Glen Morgan, Michael Dinner.

Cast: Jaime Sommers: Michelle Ryan. Jonas Bledsoe: Miquel Ferrer. Ruth Treadwell: Molly Price. Jae Kim: Will Yun Lee. Becca Sommers: Lucy Hale. Sarah Corvus: Katie Sackhoff

Leonard Nimoy and William Shatner in the original "Star Trek."

Star Trek
NBC (9/8/66–9/9/69)

Captain James T. Kirk (William Shatner) finished his five-year mission and was promoted to admiral, giving up his captain's chair for a desk. Mr. Spock

(Leonard Nimoy), meanwhile, returned to Vulcan to get in touch with himself and study logic. And Dr. McCoy (DeForest Kelley) has left Starfleet for a quieter life. But when a mysterious space cloud threatens the universe, Kirk is called back into active duty on the refurbished *Enterprise*, and he quickly recalls his old comrades to duty, including Chief Engineer Scott (James Doohan), Mr. Sulu (George Takei), Chekov (Walter Koenig), Lt. Uhura (Nichelle Nichols) and Doctor Chapel (Majel Barrett). Once the gigantic space entity, which evolved from a 1970s Voyager spacecraft, is stopped from destroying Earth, Capt. Kirk returns to his desk…

…Until a new crisis returns him to the helm of the *Enterprise*, now commanded by Capt. Spock, who has relinquished his old post to a Vulcan named Saavik (Kirstie Alley). It seems that Admiral Kirk's old flame, Dr. Carol Marcus (Bibi Besch), and their son David (Merritt Butrick) have created a missile than can take a barren planet and turn it into a lush paradise, and they think he wants them to turn it over to the Federation. The truth is they are being manipulated by Khan, an old enemy Kirk exiled to a deserted planet decades ago. Kirk defeats Khan, but at a high price–Spock quickly mindmelds with Dr. McCoy and then sacrifices his own life to save the ship. Kirk lays Spock to rest on the new world his son created, called the Genesis Planet, which is promptly declared off-limits by the Federation.

No sooner do they return to Earth than Dr. McCoy begins behaving very strangely, and is arrested by Federation officers for trying to commandeer a ship to the Genesis Planet. And Ambassador Sarek (Mark Lenard), Spock's father, pays Admiral Kirk a visit–demanding to know who his son "gave" his thoughts to before his death. Kirk realizes Spock may still be alive, and that McCoy holds what is left of Spock's mind. Violating Federation law, Kirk and his crew break McCoy out of detention, steal the *Enterprise*, and race to the Genesis Planet. Meanwhile, Saavik (Robin Curtis) and David Marcus are investigating tumultuous changes on the unstable planet, which is aging so quickly that it seems headed toward imminent disintegration. And aging along with it is Spock, who they discover is rapidly re-evolving from infant to adult. As if that weren't enough, they are kidnapped on the Genesis Planet by rogue Klingon commander Kruge (Christopher Lloyd), who ends up in a standoff with Admiral Kirk, which the Klingon breaks by killing Kirk's son. Admiral Kirk surrenders and allows the Klingons to board his ship–but our heroes beam off as the enemy is beaming aboard, and the *Enterprise* self-destructs, leaving Kirk and his crew marooned on the planet. Kirk kills Kruge in a fight, and he and his men overpower Kruge's small crew, taking over the Klingon ship and returning Spock to Vulcan, where his "being" is transferred back from McCoy in a ritualistic ceremony.

Kirk and his crew remain fugitives from justice on Vulcan during Spock's rehabilitation, while at Federation headquarters the Klingons are demanding Kirk's head. Kirk and his crew are about to return in their overhauled Klingon ship to face charges (leaving Saavik behind on Vulcan for reasons that aren't too clear) when they discover that a strange object from deep space is in Earth orbit and is radically disrupting the atmosphere in an attempt to communicate with extinct humpback whales. To save Earth, Kirk and his crew travel back through time to 1980s San Francisco to find some whales and bring them back to the future, a mission made riskier by Spock's jumbled mind, which still isn't quite together. They find the whales and bring them back, along with marine biologist Gillian Taylor (Catherine Hicks). The strange, alien object communicates something to the whales, and then leaves as mysteriously as it arrived. Kirk and his crew are tried; Kirk is demoted to captain, a penalty he is glad to accept, and is given the command of a new *Enterprise*.

Kirk, Spock, and McCoy then head off for some much deserved rest in Yosemite, when Spock's heretofore unmentioned half-brother Sybok (Laurence Luckinbill), who is able to psychically unlock people's inner turmoil and turn them into his slavelike followers, takes over a Federation outpost, kidnapping the Federation and Klingon ambassadors. Kirk and company go to the rescue, only to be overpowered by the "turned" kidnappées and have the Enterprise commandeered by Sybok, who "turns" the crew and enlists them in his quest—to break through the Forbidden Zone at the center of the galaxy and meet God, the all-powerful entity which has been communicating with him. Only Spock and Kirk are able to resist Sybok—but when the Vulcan breaks through the barrier to "Eden," Kirk agrees to help. Together, Kirk, Spock, McCoy, and Sybok face the entity, only to discover it is not God at all, but an evil alien. Sybok sacrifices himself by attempting to link with the alien and unlock its turmoil—giving McCoy and Spock the chance to escape. Kirk is unable to make it, and just when it looks like he is about to be killed by the vengeful alien, Spock saves his life.

A few years pass. Capt. Sulu, now commanding the *Excelsior*, witnesses a freak accident on a Klingon moon. The accident causes the irreversible, rapid decay of the Klingon homeworld's atmosphere, forcing the Klingons into abandoning their home for a new one. Seeing an opportunity for peace, the Federation sends Spock to negotiate an accord with the Klingons in exchange for finding their longtime enemies a new home in Federation space. The Klingons are sending their special envoy Chairman Gorkon (David Warner) to Earth for talks, and Capt. Kirk and the *Enterprise* have been selected to escort him. Kirk still hates the Klingons, blaming them all for the death of his son.

In space, the *Enterprise* meets with the Klingon ship carrying Chairman Gorkon, which is commanded by Chang (Christopher Plummer), a Shakespeare-quoting warrior who clearly will miss the hostilities between the two worlds. No sooner have the Klingons returned to their ship than the *Enterprise* seemingly opens fire on them. Two assassins, in Federation space suits, beam onto the Klingon ship and shoot Gorkon. Kirk, horrified, beams over to the Klingon ship with Dr. McCoy, who is unable to save Gorkon's life. A furious Chang arrests Kirk and McCoy, and they are sentenced by a Klingon court to life in exile on an icy prison planet.

Spock and the crew conduct an investigation of their own and determine that a cloaked Klingon ship was the real culprit, but that someone on the *Enterprise* was working with them. The Federation, meanwhile, arranges for peace talks to continue and Kirk and McCoy engineer an escape. Kirk and McCoy are nearly killed, but Spock rescues them at the last minute and together they discover that Spock's Vulcan protégé Valeris (Kim Cattrall) is the spy on board, working in conjunction with Chang and others upset at the prospect of peace. The *Enterprise*, assisted by the *Excelsior*, races to the secret negotiation site to prevent another assassination from occurring.

Once again saving civilization as we know it, Kirk, McCoy, and Mr. Spock are finally ready to retire, and the *Enterprise* is decommissioned...until the day when a new *Enterprise*, and a new crew, can explore strange new worlds.

Some time later, retired shipmates Kirk, Scotty and Chekov are on hand for the first voyage of the Enterprise-B when it encounters a mysterious energy beam that slices a hole in the ship. Kirk is sucked into deep space... and is killed.

Eighty years later, an elderly Dr. McCoy is on hand to christen another new starship *Enterprise* and its crew: Capt. Jean-Luc Picard (Patrick Stewart), his first officer Will Riker (Jonathan Frakes), android Lt. Commander Data (Brent Spiner), blind navigator Geordi La Forge (LeVar Burton), Klingon Lt. Worf (Michael Dorn), and security officer Tasha Yar (Denise Crosby). Other officers include Counselor Deanna Troi (Marina Sirtis), a Betazoid empath who is the ship's psychological expert, and Dr. Beverly Crusher (Gates McFadden) and her son, Ensign Will Crusher (Wil Wheaton), whose father was killed on a mission with Picard. Later they are joined by Transporter Chief O'Brien (Colm Meaney), barkeep Guinan (Whoopi Goldberg) and, briefly, Dr. Kate Pulaski (Diana Muldaur) when Dr. Crusher goes on an extended mission for Starfleet.

Shortly after the *Enterprise-D* begins its new mission, Tasha Yar is killed by an evil entity resembling an oil slick and is replaced as security officer by Lt. Worf, though she returns later in a bizarre time warp and then is hurled into the past, where she is eventually captured by Romulans and bears a half–Romulan child who grows up to become Picard's arch adversary.

While taking Ambassador Sarek, something of a legend in the Federation, to oversee delicate talks with an alien race, Picard discovers the aging Vulcan is suffering from a serious, Alzheimer's-like disorder that breaks down the mental barrier the Vulcans mantain around their emotions. Sarek is forced to meld with Picard, transferring his troubled soul into the captain until negotiations are complete. As a result, Picard has a special bond with the Vulcan–one that comes to the fore when Sarek dies and his son, Ambassador Spock, disappears and is found to be on the planet Romulus. Picard and Data, disguised as Romulans, find Spock and discover the rogue ambassador is attempting to forge a peaceful alliance with the Romulans as he once did with the Klingons. But he is playing into a trap, an attempt by Tasha Yar's Romulan child to invade Vulcan. Spock, Picard, and Data foil the plot, but Spock decides to remain on Romulan, working with the Romulan underground to foster understanding between the two worlds.

Picard and his crew later find Scotty, or rather his dissembled molecules, locked in the transporter machine of a crashed spaceship, where he has been held in limbo for nearly a century. They free him and send him off in a shuttle-craft to enjoy his belated retirement.

Some years after that, the crew of the Enterprise encounters the same energy beam that killed Captain Kirk...and a man named Dr. Trolian Soran, who is obsessed with entering an extradimensional space called The Nexus that is associated with that deadly energy disturbance. For complicated reasons, Soran's obsession endangers the safety of an entire galaxy.

Many events ensue, including the destruction of the *Enterprise*. Along the way, Capt. Picard is sucked into the Nexus, where he encounters Capt. Kirk, still very much alive, and living in an alternate reality. Picard convinces Kirk to escape with him from the Nexus with him to battle Soran. Kirk agrees… and manages to save a planet from destruction…but sacrifices his life to do it.

In the year 2362, or thereabouts, Mr. Spock attempts to prevent a supernova from swallowing the planet Romulus. He tries to use "red matter" to create a black hole to consume the supernova…but the plan backfires and Romulus is destroyed. Spock's vessel, and a Romulan mining craft called the Narada, are sucked into the black hole and hurled back 129 years. The commander of the Narada, a Romulan named Nero, strands Spock on an ice planet so the Vulcan can watch the Romulans destroy the planet Vulcan with the "red matter" in revenge.

The planet Vulcan is destroyed, altering the past and future, and leads to Young Spock (Zachary Quinto) and Young Kirk (Chris Pine) and the rest of the Enterprise crew to battling Narada to Earth from destruction. The "old" Spock with the handful of survivors of Vulcan to colonize another planet as the new Vulcan homeworld while the Young Spock sets out on new adventures with the crew of the *Enterprise*, making the past new once again.

Background

With "Star Trek," Gene Roddenberry created a new dramatic form for television that was extraordinarily flexible. While most series inevitably are boxed in to some degree by the limitations of their concepts, "Star Trek" was an idea with surprisingly few limitations–just about arty story could be told, just about any idea explored, and still fall into the boundaries of the series.

"Star Trek" convinced Roddenberry that with science fiction, "you can exercise your imagination more. I fell in love with it."

And so did a group of dedicated fans who, when low-rated "Star Trek" was canceled after two seasons, came together and rallied NBC with a massive letter-writing campaign. The network changed its usually intractable mind and gave "Star Trek" a third season. But the ratings failed to improve, and the series was canceled again, seemingly for good. The 79-episode run was considered by the industry, and even by Roddenberry, as an expensive failure. It was consigned to rerun oblivion.

But that was not the end. "Star Trek" had been canceled, but it was not off the air. The reruns were more successful than the primetime series, and the number of fans was growing.

The ever-growing legion of Trekkers held countless conventions around the world, gobbled up thousands of home-made fanzines and trinkets, and wrote their own amateur "Star Trek" poetry, songs and novels, "even some S&M and homosexual things about Kirk and Spock," said Gene Roddenberry, a man who remained surprised by what his television series had wrought. His office at Paramount was full of "Star Trek" books, records, models, and the like, but that just scratched the surface. "Are you kidding? I've got boxes of stuff, stuff you'd have to be drunk to invent." The amazing array of "Star Trek" memorabilia, however, also included some serious works of his own, including a book (*The Making of Star Trek*) and a record album (*Inside Star Trek*).

The unprecedented fan interest prompted Filmmation and NBC to revive "Star Trek"–as a cartoon. What "Star Trek" did for SF drama in the 1960s, it did for Saturday morning cartoons in the '70s. "Star Trek" became the first canceled network series to be revived in animation–something of an intellectual oddity among "Scooby Doo," the "Far Out Space Nuts," and "Lancelot Link: Secret Chimp." The concept proved durable in any form, and the writers, many of whom had written for the original series, and the original cast members rose to the occasion. It didn't go unnoticed, or unrewarded. The series won an Emmy in 1974 as "Outstanding Children's Series."

A few years later, the success of *Star Wars* at the box office convinced Paramount executives that they could capitalize on the sudden popularity of science fiction with a new "Star Trek" television series. Paramount executive Barry Diller envisioned the new series as the cornerstone of the studio's own ad hoc television network. But the studio was a bit ahead of its time on both fronts–it would be another ten years before Paramount's new "Star Trek" television series, or Diller's fourth network, would be launched.

The revived series became a movie instead, a decade after its demise. And not just any film, but a big-budget milestone, the first time a television series had been revived as a theatrical film. Although 1979's *Star Trek: The Motion Picture* delivered on many levels, it left the fans—and Roddenberry, the film's executive producer—somewhat dissatisfied. The movie, though it brought the crew back together, lacked the charm and humor of the original series.

Roddenberry learned there was a critical difference between the way television shows and movies are made. "Although 'Star Trek' was my baby, in films it's the director who is in control. I found no one was paying attention to what I wanted. The movie reflected that. I couldn't get through to anybody that it should be a family ensemble."

Nevertheless, the film was a success and sparked five more sequels, the first of which, *Star Trek II: The Wrath of Khan*, was another milestone—the first time a television episode spawned a theatrical sequel. Yet, in Roddenberry's estimation, it wasn't until *Star Trek IV: The Voyage Home* that "they finally got it right." The theatrical series featuring the original cast presumably ended with *Star Trek VI: The Undiscovered Country*, in which the *Enterprise* is decommissioned and its officers retire. Kirk later appeared, only to die, in the first of four *Star Trek: The Next Generation* feature films.

In all, the *Star Trek* films represented still another first: the first time a television series evolved into a theatrical series.

Roddenberry opted to fall back to the role of consultant on the later films. "The only thing I ever insisted on was that they keep the 'Star Trek' philosophy. I told [writer/producer] Harve Bennett that if they ever land on a planet and start zapping creatures just because they look different, I call a press conference." He credited Bennett with "keeping it alive" and was proud of writer/director/actor Leonard Nimoy's contribution. "I love it. I knew someone from inside would know how to make it work. Leonard knew the band of brothers idea worked in the series and he made it work in the movies."

Despite the new big-budget movies, the original television series was not forgotten. Eventually, all 79 episodes of the original series, and later the animated shows, were released into home video.

Even if the "Star Trek" story had ended there, it would have been unprecedented. It didn't. In 1986, fueled by the success of the movies, Roddenberry entered the sort of time warp the *Enterprise* crew might encounter—he found himself back at Paramount, doing a television series called "Star Trek," albeit "The Next Generation."

The new series was born in talks with Fox Broadcasting Co., the upstart fourth network headed by Barry Diller that was about to premiere with a weekend of original programming. Once again, Diller saw "Star Trek," and the built-in audience it brought with it, as a natural cornerstone. Paramount Television opted instead to do the series on its own for first-run syndication—where studios and stations were boldly going where they had safely gone before, relying almost entirely on revivals and remakes of old shows.

To give the new project credibility—both to fickle stations and to wary fans—Paramount Television offered Roddenberry the series, and a chance to do whatever he wanted. Best of all, "when I asked who the censor was going to be, they said 'you,'" said Roddenberry. "That did it."

It would begin with a two-hour movie, followed by 24 hour-long episodes budgeted at a whopping $1 million plus each. A big gamble, to be sure, but a small risk when balanced against the potential rewards. Even with Roddenberry's involvement, station owners, fans, and the original cast were skeptical.

"It's a mystery to me why they are doing it. I assume Paramount thinks they can hold onto the 'Star Trek' phenomenon. There's no doubt we can't go on forever so they're trying a way to keep it going," said DeForest Kelley. "But there's only one 'Star Trek,' and that's ours. I don't think they can come in with a new 'Star Trek' cast and ever recapture the feeling of the 'Star Trek' that has been or the one we've got going now. When that is gone, it's gone."

"I just regret they are calling it 'Star Trek,' when we know what it is, which is the characters," said James Doohan. "They are trying to fool the public, and that's bad business."

"I don't feel good about the new series," said William Shatner. "I think without the cast as we know it, and not in the time as we know it, it's hard to understand why they are calling it 'Star Trek.' In addition, there's the risk of over-exposure."

But they were all glad to be wrong. "Star Trek: The Next Generation" became, perhaps, as popular as the original, and certainly more successful, outdistancing its namesake in the number of episodes produced and ushering in a whole new generation of fans. And first Kelley, then Majel Barrett, Mark Lenard, Leonard Nimoy, and James Doohan would show up in guest appearances on the series.

Behind the scenes, "Star Trek: The Next Generation" was beset by a constant turnover of creative talent, going through a dozen writer/producers before finally settling down somewhat in its fourth and fifth years under the guidance of co-executive producers Michael Piller and Rick Berman. Although the show relied on all-new adventures, the second episode was a sequel to an original "Star Trek" show, and several scripts drafted for the aborted "Star Trek II" series were eventually used, albeit in extensively rewritten form, for the new series. But skeptical fans came to love the "Next Generation" almost as much as what came to be known as "Classic Trek" among Trekkers. Three more "Star Trek" series followed: "Star Trek: Deep Space Nine," "Star Trek: Voyager" and "Star Trek: Enterprise."

At the time of Roddenberry's death in 1991, "Star Trek" had never been more popular. While the cast, with the exceptions of Shatner and Nimoy, have toiled in virtual obscurity since the demise of the original "Star Trek," "the fans have kept us stars throughout all these years," said Nichelle Nichols.

When the credits roll on a "Star Trek" movie, the crowd cheers the names as if they were De Niro, Streep, and Redford rather than Shatner, Koenig, or Takei. Unfortunately, that adulation and stardom hasn't transferred to other work the actors have done.

Many members of the cast have made a living speaking at conventions or in merchandising, which came in handy when acting jobs, for some, turned out to be few and far between. Nichelle Nichols has a mail-order album called *Uhura Sings*. Leonard Nimoy cut an album of songs, including "Star Trek" tunes, and penned the book *I Am Not Spock*. Shatner also recorded an album and tried his hand as a novelist. Walter Koenig wrote a *Star Trek: The Motion Picture* diary. That's just a few.

To the fans, Roddenberry will always be the beloved "Great Bird of the Galaxy," a term actually coined as a joke by series producer Robert Justman. And everyone who has ever written for or appeared in the show is a certifiable superstar—but, for the most part, just in the so-called "Star Trek" universe.

But that "universe" is every bit as large and diverse as the word implies. "Star Trek" is available in nearly every entertainment medium. New "Star Trek" series are continuing on television, in feature films, in comics, in books, and on audio cassettes. The show's reach goes beyond the pages of *TV Guide* or the dollars collected at the toy stores and box offices. The first space shuttle was christened *Enterprise*, and the original *Enterprise* model hangs in the Smithsonian along with other national treasures.

Roddenberry was often asked what made the show so beloved, why it inspired such devotion. He credited the show's optimistic view of the future. "It's not so much about any incredible artistic perceptiveness on my part than it is the fact that, when I was very young, I was handicapped for many years," he said. "I was stuck in a dark room and not always too happy. I turned to books, and I think that's where a lot of 'Star Trek' came from, saying to myself, 'Someday there will be a better world, a world that sees the beauty that's in me and not these gawky arms and legs and the snot running out of my nose. Our fans, particularly our handicapped fans, really live for the fact we are saying it doesn't matter if you don't have any legs, it's not a real measurement of you."

Perhaps some of the devotion is simply respect. "Star Trek," even as a cartoon, never played down to its audience. Roddenberry always assumed the viewers were intelligent, an assessment not often shared by network executives and television producers.

But James Doohan believes there is nothing intellectual about it. "All I can tell you is it has some kind of magic. That's the only answer, no matter what anybody says about scripts, hope for future, or great characters. I say it has to be magic."

Star Trek: The Motion Picture

Paramount Pictures. Theatrical. (1979). Director: Robert Wise. Producer: Gene Roddenberry, Jon Povill. Screenplay: Harold Livingston. From a story by Alan Dean Foster. Music: Jerry Goldsmith. Star Trek theme by Alexander Courage.

Cast. Admiral James T. Kirk: William Shatner. Mr. Spock: Leonard Nimoy. Dr. Leonard "Bones" McCoy: DeForest Kelley. Commander Pavel Chekov: Walter Koenig. Commander Sulu: George Takei. Engineer Montgomery Scott: James Doohan. Commander Uhura: Nichelle Nichols. Dr. Chapel: Majel Barrett. Captain Will Decker: Stephen Collins. Ilia: Persis Khambata. Klingon Captain: Mark Lenard. Janice Rand: Grace Lee Whitney. Commander Branch: David Gautreaux.

A scene from *Star Trek II: The. Wrath of Khan.*

Star Trek II: The Wrath of Khan

Paramount Pictures. Theatrical. (1982). Director: Nicholas Meyer. Producer: Gene Roddenberry, Harve Bennett, William F. Phillips. Robert Sallin. Screenplay: Jack B. Sowards. Story by Harve Bennett & Jack B. Sowards. Music: James Horner

Cast. Admiral James T. Kirk: William Shatner. Captain Spock: Leonard Nimoy. Dr. Leonard "Bones" McCoy: DeForest Kelley. Commander Pavel Chekov: Walter Koenig. Commander Sulu: George Takei. Engineer Montgomery Scott: James Doohan. Commander Uhura: Nichelle Nichols. Lt. Saavik: Kirstie Alley. Khan: Ricardo Montalban. David Marcus: Merritt Butrick. Carol Marcus: Bibi Besch. Terrell: Paul Winfield. Preston: Ike Eisenmann. Beach: Paul Kent.

Star Trek III: The Search for Spock

Paramount Pictures. Theatrical. (1984). Director: Leonard Nimoy. Producer: Gene Roddenberry, Harve Bennett, Gary Nardino. Ralph Winter. Screenplay: Harve Bennett. Music: James Horner

Cast. Admiral James T. Kirk: William Shatner. Captain Spock: Leonard Nimoy. Dr. Leonard "Bones" McCoy: DeForest Kelley. Commander Pavel Chekov: Walter Koenig. Commander Sulu: George Takei. Engineer Montgomery Scott: James Doohan. Commander Uhura: Nichelle Nichols. Lt. Saavik: Robin Curtis. Commander Kruge: Christopher Lloyd. Ambassador Sarek: Mark Lenard. Amanda: Jane Wyatt. David Marcus: Merritt Butrick. Young Spock: Christian Slater. Mr. Adventure: Scott McGinnis. Foster: Phil Morris. Admiral Morrow: Robert Hooks. Maltz: John Larroquette. Klingon Gunner: Branscombe Richmond. Capt. Styles: James B. Sikking. First Officer: Miguel Ferrer.

Star Trek IV: The Voyage Home

Paramount Pictures. Theatrical. (1986). Director: Leonard Nimoy. Producer: Gene Roddenberry, Harve Bennett, Brooke Breton, Ralph Winter. Screenplay: Steve Meerson & Peter Krikes and Harve Bennett & Nicholas Meyer. Music: Leonard Rosenman

Cast. Admiral James T. Kirk: William Shatner. Captain Spock: Leonard Nimoy. Dr. Leonard "Bones" McCoy: DeForest Kelley. Commander Pavel Chekov: Walter Koenig. Commander Sulu: George Takei. Engineer Montgomery Scott: James Doohan. Commander Uhura: Nichelle Nicohols. Lt. Saavik: Robin Curtis. Dr. Gillian Taylor: Catherine Hicks. Ambassador Sarek: Mark Lenard. Klingon Ambassador: John Schuck. Admiral Cartwright: Brock Peters. Amanda: Jane Wyatt. Sarek: Mark Lenard. Commander Rand: Grace Lee Whitney. Commander Chapel: Majel Barrett.

Star Trek V: The Final Frontier

Paramount Pictures. Theatrical. (1989). Director: William Shatner. Producer: Gene Roddenberry, Harve Bennett. Ralph Winter. Brooke Breton. Screenplay: David Loughery. Story by William Shatner & Harve Bennett & David Loughery. Music: Jerry Goldsmith

Cast. Capt. James T. Kirk: William Shatner. Capt. Spock: Leonard Nimoy. Dr. Leonard "Bones" McCoy: DeForest Kelley. Commander Pavel Chekov: Walter Koenig. Commander Sulu: George Takei. Engineer Montgomery Scott: James Doohan. Commander Uhura: Nichelle Nichols. Sybok: Laurence Luckinbill. God: George Murdock. Sir John Talbott: David Warner. Young Sarek: Jonathan Simpson. Starfleet Chief of Staff: Harve Bennett. McCoy's Father: Bill Quinn.

Star Trek VI: The Undiscovered Country

Paramount Pictures. Theatrical. (1991). Director: Nicholas Meyer. Producer: Leonard Nimoy, Brooke Breton, Ralph Winter, Steven-Charles Joffe. Screenplay: Nicholas Meyer & Denny Martin Flinn. From a story by Lawrence Konner, Mark Rosenthal and Leonard Nimoy. Music: Cliff Eidelman

Cast. Captain James T. Kirk: William Shatner. Captain Spock: Leonard Nimoy. Dr. Leonard "Bones" McCoy: DeForest Kelley. Commander Pavel Chekov: Walter Koenig. Capt. Sulu: George Takei. Engineer Montgomery Scott: James Doohan. Commander Uhura: Nichelle Nichols. Lt. Valeris: Kim Cattrall. Commander Chang: Christopher Plummer. Chairman Gorkon: David Warner. Colonel Worf: Michael Dorn. Sarek: Mark Lenard. Admiral Cartwright: Brock Peters. President: Kurtwood Smith. Klingon Ambassador: John Schuck. Rand: Grace Lee Whitney. Chief in Command: Leon Russom. Azetbur: Rosanna DeSoto. Col. West: Rene Auberjonois. (With a cameo by Christian Slater.)

"Star Trek: The Next Generation"

Paramount Television Syndicated. 60 minutes, 176 episodes (9/28/87–5/23/94). Production Company: Paramount Television. Executive Producers: Gene Roddenberry, Rick Berman, Maurice Hurley, Michael Piller, Jeri Taylor. Producers: David Livingston, Robert Lewin, Richard Manning & Hans Beimler, Peter Lauritson, Brannon Braga, Burton Armus, Frank Abatemarco, D.C Fontana, Robert McCullough, Herbert Wright, Lee Sheldon, Ronald D. Moore, Joe Menosky. Wendy Neuss. Merri D. Howard. Story Editors: Hannah Louise Shearer, David Gerrold, J. Larry Carroll, David Bennett Carren, Ira Steven Behr, Tracy Torme, Melinda M. Snodgrass. Theme: Jerry Goldsmith, Alexander Courage. Music: Dennis McCarthy, Ron Jones, Jay Chattaway

Cast. Capt. Jean-Luc Picard: Patrick Stewart. Commander William Riker: Jonathan Frakes. Lt. Worf: Michael Dorn. Lt. Commander Data: Brent Spiner. Counselor Deanna Troi: Marina Sirtis. Ensign Wesley Crusher: Wil Wheaton. Lt. Geordi La Forge: LeVar Burton. Dr. Beverly Crusher: Gates McFadden. Tasha Yar: Denise Crosby. Dr. Pulaski: Diana Muldaur. Chief Miles O'Brien: Colm Meaney. Guiñan: Whoopi Goldberg. Lwaxana Troi: Majel Barrett. Q: John de Lancie.

Star Trek Generations (aka "Star Trek VII")

Paramount Pictures. Theatrical (1994) Director: David Carson. Producers: Rick Berman, Peter Lauritson, Bernard Williams. Writers: Rick Berman, Ronald D. Moore, Brannon Braga. Music: Dennis McCarthy

Cast: Capt. Jean-Luc Picard: Patrick Stewart. Commander William Riker: Jonathan Frakes. Lt. Worf: Michael Dorn. Lt. Commander Data: Brent Spiner. Counselor Deanna Troi: Marina Sirtis. Ensign Wesley Crusher: Wil Wheaton. Lt. Geordi La Forge: LeVar Burton. Dr. Beverly Crusher: Gates McFadden. Chief Miles O'Brien: Colm Meaney. Guiñan: Whoopi Goldberg. Soran: Malcolm McDowell. Admiral Kirk: Willam Shatner. Scotty: James Doohan. Chekov: Walter Koenig. Capt. Harriman: Alan Ruck. Demora: Jacqueline Kim. Science officer: Jenette Goldstein

Leonard Nimoy as Spock in the 2009 "reboot" of "Star Trek"

Star Trek

Paramount Pictures. Bad Robot. Theatrical. (2009) Director: J.J. Abrams. Producers: J.J. Abrams, Bryan Burk. Damon Lindelof, Jeffery Chernov, Alex Kurtzman, Roberto Orci. Writers: Alex Kurtzman, Roberto Orci, based on "Star Trek" by Gene Roddenberry. Music: Michael Giacchino.

Cast: Capt. Kirk: Chris Pine. Mr. Spock: Zachary Quinto. Spock Prime: Leonard Nimoy. Nero: Eric Bana. Capt. Pike: Bruce Greenwood. Dr. McCoy: Karl Urban. Scotty: Simon Pegg. Mr. Sulu: John Cho. Chekov: Anton Yelchin. Sarek: Ben Cross. Amanda: Winona Ryder. Uhura: Zoe Saldana. George Kirk: Chris Hemsworth. Winona Kirk: Jennifer Morrison. Young Spock: Jacob Kogan. Admiral Barnett: Tyler Perry.

See also "Star Trek" in the appendix.

Streets of San Francisco
ABC (9/16/72–6/23/77)

Lt. Mike Stone has been promoted to captain, and he has two new protégés—aggressive Sarah Burns (Debrah Farentino), the daughter of a judge (William Daniels), and a family man David O'Connor (Conor O'Farrell), the son of a cop. Stone's old protégé Steve Keller (Michael Douglas) has become a criminology professor and is married to Ann, who is also a professor.

But when Keller fails to show up for a dinner date, Stone suspects the worst—and discovers that Carl Murchison, a man he and Keller sent to prison, is out on parole and has strangled Keller. Murchison kidnaps Stone's daughter Jean (now a married psychologist with two kids) and uses her as bait to lure Stone to a showdown.

Background

This was supposed to be the first of three "Streets of San Francisco" television movies. Although this one did well, and a second script, tentatively entitled "A Question of Loyalty," was written by executive producer/writer William Robert Yates, no further movies were made. CBS did commission a "Streets of San Francisco" reboot in 2005, from writer Sheldon Turner, producer Robert Port, and director Simon West, but it didn't go forward. That said, the characters live on in print. The TV series was based on three novels by Carolyn Weston, which were republished in 2015 by Brash Books, which also commissioned new books in the series by Robin Burcel, a police officer and acclaimed crime fiction author.

"Back to the Streets of San Francisco"

NBC TV movie. Two hours (1/27/92). Production Company: Aaron Spelling Productions. Executive Producers: Aaron Spelling, William Robert Yates, E. Duke Vincent, Melissa Goldsmith. Director: Mel Damski. Producer: Diana Karew. Writer: William Robert Yates. Based on characters created by Carolyn Weston. Series developed by Edward Hume. Music: Patrick Williams.

Cast. Capt. Mike Stone: Karl Malden. Inspector Sarah Burns: Debrah Farentino. Inspector David O'Connor: Conor O'Farrell. Jean Stone: Darleen Carr. Inspector Charlie Walker: Carl Lumbly. Henry Brown: Paul Benjamin. Judge Julius Burns: William Daniels. Sam Hendrix: Robert Parnell. Carl Murchison: Nick Scoggin.

That's My Mama!
ABC (9/4/74–12/14/75)

Clifton Curtis (Clifton Davis) is a Washington, D.C., barber trying to run his business, and his life, without the constant intrusion of his pushy mother Eloise "Mama" Curtis (Theresa Merritt). Which is a lot easier now, since he has moved to Alaska to become a D.J. at KOLD radio.

Clifton has sold his business to Clarence "Junior" Russell (Ted Lange), the street philosopher turned lawyer who converts the barbershop into an office and hires Mama as his secretary. This arrangement is handy, since Mama's house adjoins the shop. It also means Clarence becomes a de facto member of the family, which includes Mama's ultra-straight son-in-law Leonard (Lisle Wilson), her daughter Tracy (Daphne Maxwell), and her grandchildren (Tony Carothers, Alexandra Simmons). And there is one other regular visitor, Clarence's inept investigator Deuce (Timothy Stack).

And although they are in town only for a visit, Mama's nephew Roger Thomas (Ernest Thomas) and his wife Nadine (Anne-Marie Johnson) show up every so often from California for a little vacation.

Background
"When we first heard about it, we thought it was a joke," says Jay Moriarty, co-producer with Mike Milligan of "That's My Mama Now!" "However, 'What's Happening Now!' sounded like a joke, but it's number one in first-run syndication. That show is a joke, but a very successful joke."

Moriarty and Milligan, who were supervising producers of "What's Happening Now!" were asked by Columbia Pictures Television to develop a pilot for a continuation of "That's My Mama" as one of its episodes.

Obviously, there were no hordes of eager fans clamoring for new "That's My Mama" episodes. But Columbia had 37 episodes sitting on a shelf and hoped to parlay the success of "What's Happening Now" into a spinoff and, Moriarty said, "make some bucks by adding to the episodes they already have."

Theresa Merritt, Ted Lange, and Lisle Wilson recreated their roles from the original series. Not that anyone would remember. Even so, the reasoning was that it's better to revive an old show, even a bomb, than "to explain a whole new series," said Milligan. "At least this has a track record."

Besides, "'That's My Mama Now' is a whole different show," he added. "It's 'The Ted Lange Show,' really. He's a recognizable face with a big following."

Apparently it was a big enough following to get "That's My Mama Now!" sold.

"That's My Mama Now!"

Syndicated pilot. 30 minutes (1987). Production Company: Columbia Pictures Television. Producers: Jay Moriarty, Mike Milligan.

Cast. Clarence Russell, Jr.: Ted Lange. Eloise Curtis: Theresa Merritt. Leonard Taylor: Lisle Wilson. Tracy Taylor: Daphne Maxwell. Deuce: Timothy Stack. Lenny: Tony Carothers. Honey: Alexandra Simmons. Roger Thomas: Ernest Thomas. Nadine Thomas: Anne-Marie Johnson.

Tightrope
CBS (9/8/59–9/13/60)

Nick Stone (Mike Connors) is an undercover cop who infiltrates the mob and brings down crooks without ever blowing his cover.

Background

Producers Clarence Green and Russell Rouse really believed in their show. As soon as it was canceled by CBS, they were rallying for its return. They tried to mount a new version a year later, and the year after that they shot another pilot, this time for ABC. Screen Gems attempted it one more time-ten years later, with "Man on a String," loosely based on "Tightrope" and featuring Christopher George as an undercover agent. It wasn't until "Wiseguy," a Stephen J. Cannell series, that the concept finally got a shot on weekly television.

"The Expendables"

ABC pilot. 60 minutes (9/27/62). Production Company: Screen Gems. Producers: Clarence Green, Russell Rouse.

Cast. Nick Stone: Mike Connors. Also: Zachary Scott, Dina Merrill.

The Untouchables
ABC (10/15/59–9/10/63)

World War II is over. Prohibition has been lifted. Capone is dead, and Chicago has become a war zone where the remaining gangsters are battling for control. Elliot Ness, who has since married, comes out of retirement when one of his old Untouchables, falsely accused of corruption, is murdered. Teaming up with the murdered man's son (Jack Coleman), a Chicago cop, Ness pursues gangster Art Molto (Philip Bosco) and his hotheaded son Bobby (Anthony De Sando) and brings them down, clearing his friend's name in the process.

Background

Although Paramount enjoyed box office success with a theatrical version of "The Untouchables," the film really owed nothing to the television series. It was not until 1991 that Robert Stack returned for a television sequel to the series that made him famous. One can forgive the absence of Walter Winchell's narration—and the unwillingness to hire someone to copy the late journalist's distinctive voice. But in subtracting the Untouchables themselves ("Youngblood! Rico!"), the Nelson Riddle theme ("duuuuumm, dee dum dum dum dum"), the chilling violence, the flamboyant villains, and any evidence of the series's unique style and tone, the studio created a rather flat and unsatisfying reprise. In 1993, Paramount launched a new "Untouchables" series for first-run syndication modeled more after the Brian De Palma movie version of Ness' story than the Robert Stack television series.

"The Return of Elliot Ness"

NBC TV movie. Two hours (11/10/91). Production Company: Michael Filerman Productions. Director: James Contner. Executive Producer: Michael Filerman. Producers: Joseph B. Wallenstein, John Danylkiw, Michael Petryni. Writer: Michael Petryni. Music: Lee Holdridge.

Cast. Elliot Ness: Robert Stack. Marty Labine: Frank Adamson. Gil Labine: Jack Coleman. Roger Finn: Charles Durning. Madeline: Lisa Hartman. Art Molto: Phillip Bosco. Bobby Molto: Anthony De Sando. Also: Michael Copeman, Ron Lea, Frank Adamson, Shaun Austin Olsen, J. Winston Carroll, George Chuvalo, Kay Hawtrey, Michael Kirby, Dwight Bacquie, Rummy Bishop, Walker Boone, Frank Canino, David Clement, Cindy Cook, Shaun Cowan, Tony Craig, Richard Curnock, Daniel De Santo.

Wanted Dead or Alive
CBS (9/6/58–3/29/61)

Josh Randall (Steve McQueen) was a bounty hunter in the old west who carried a special Winchester carbine. His great grandson Nick (Rutger Hauer) follows in the same tradition, using whatever high-tech weaponry he can find. He's a former CIA agent turned bounty hunter who finds himself pursued by, and pursuing, international terrorist Malak Al Rahim (Gene Simmons).

Wanted Dead or Alive

New World Pictures. Theatrical. (1986). Production Company: New World Pictures, Balcor Film Investors, Arthur Sarkissian Productions. Executive

Producers: Arthur M. Sarkissian. Producers: Robert C. Peters, Barry Bernardi. Director: Gary Sherman. Writers: Michael Patrick Goodman, Brian Taggert, Gary Sherman.

Cast. Nick Randall: Rutger Hauer. Malak Al Rahim: Gene Simmons. Walker: Robert Guillaume. Danny Quintz: William Russ. Terry: Mel Harris. Loise Quint: Susan McDonald. John Lipton: Jerry Hardin. Patrick Danoby: Hugh Gillian. Dave Henderson: Robert Harper. Robert Aziz: Eli Danker. Farnsworth: Dennis Burkley. Mrs. Farnsworth: DeeDee Rescher.

We Got It Made
NBC (9/8/83–3/30/84)

When roommates David Tucker (Matt McCoy, John Hillner), a busy lawyer, and Jay Bostwick (Tom Villard), an irreverent importer, hire a sexy, naïve live-in maid named Mickey (Teri Copley), they are unprepared for the impact it will have on their lives—or the ire it will provoke with their girlfriends Beth (Bonnie Urseth), a kindergarten teacher, and Clauda (Stephanie Kramer). The girlfriends are gone now, but Mickey remains. They now have a cop (Ron Karabotsos) and his young son (Lance Wilson White) living across the hall.

Background

This was Fred Silverman's attempt to do for NBC what "Three's Company" did for ABC. Three years after "We Got It Made" bombed on NBC, he tried to revive it in syndication, where standards for sitcoms are lower, stations are hungrier for fresh product, and production companies are able to turn losers with a virtually worthless number of deficit-financed episodes into bankable assets by using "barter syndication" to produce a 100-show package.

"Is it better to redo 'We Got It Made' and call it 'Everybody Wants to Get Laid'?" said Norman Horowitz, former president of MGM/UA Telecommunications. "People would rather buy something they know, that gives them comfort, than something innovative and different."

But no one was buying this show. It survived just one season.

"We Got It Made"

Syndicated. 30 minutes, 22 episodes (1987). Production Company: Intermedia Productions, MGM/UA Television. Executive Producers: Fred Silverman & Gordon Farr. Supervising Producers: Casey Keller, Richard Albrecht. Creators: Gordon Farr, Lynne Farr.

Cast. Jay Bostwick: Tom Villard. David Tucker: John Hillner. Mickey MacKenzie: Teri Copley. Max Papavasilios: Ron Karabotsos. Max Junior: Lance Wilson White.

The Westerner
NBC (1/6/61–7/7/61)

Dave Blasingame (Brian Keith) was a drifter who roamed the Old West with his dog Brown and a wily con man named Burgundy Smith (John Dehner). A hundred years later, their descendants are apparently doing exactly the same thing. Dave Blasingame (Lee Marvin) is a drifter roaming the backroads with his dog, also named Brown, and wily con man Burgundy Smith (Keenan Wynn).

Background
Sam Peckinpah's highly regarded "Westerner" was prematurely canceled, he felt, because it was too adult. For whatever reason, it was a fine show that should have continued—and Peckinpah decided to give it a second try, this time bringing his characters to a contemporary setting. The unsold pilot, entitled "The Losers," aired on "The Dick Powell Theatre" to little notice and is remembered only as an unusual footnote to an unusual series.

"The Losers"

NBC pilot. 60 minutes (1/15/63). Available on home video. Production Company: Four Star. Director: Sam Peckinpah. Executive Producer: Dick Powell. Producers: Sam Peckinpah, Bruce Geller, Bernard L. Kowalski.

Writer: Bruce Geller. Story by Geller and Peckinpah. Creator: Sam Peckinpah. Music: Herschel Burke Gilbert.

Cast. Dave Blasingame: Lee Marvin. Burgundy Smith: Keenan Wynn. Melissa: Rosemary Clooney. Blind Johnny: Adam Lazarre. Tim: Michael Davis. Mr. Anston: Mike Mazurki. Gregory: Dub Taylor. Jean: Carmen Phillips. Deidre: Elaine Walker. Farr: Jack Perkins. Mulana: Charles Horvath. Monroe: Paul Stader. Frank Davis: Kelly Thordsen. Isaiah: Russ Brown.

What's Happening!
ABC (8/5/76–4/28/79)

Roger Thomas (Ernest Thomas) always wanted to be a writer, even when he was living at home with his mother (Mabel King) and his wisecracking sister Dee (Danielle Spencer).

Now, six years later, he is living at home again, only now he is a successful novelist and happily married to Nadine (Anne-Marie Johnson). Dee is off at college, and his mother has remarried and moved, giving him the house, which becomes a regular hang-out for his old friends Rerun (Fred Berry), Dwayne (Haywood Nelson) and Shirley (Shirley Hemphill). Rerun has become a car salesman and shares an apartment with Dwayne, who programs computers and later decides to open his own magic shop. Shirley is no longer a waitress at the local diner; she co-owns it with Roger, who decides with Nadine to take in a foster child (Reina King).

Background

Out of all the first-run, syndicated sitcoms in the 1980s, "What's Happening Now!" was one of the first, and easily one of the most successful. It also was one of the very few to arise out of genuine viewer interest—the off-network reruns proved so popular that Columbia revived the show. And when "What's Happening" did well, it prompted a lot of other studios to peek into their vaults to see what short-lived series could be dressed up as new. Although most of the original cast returned, Fred Berry left the show early in its run over a salary dispute.

Haywood Nelson, Anne-Mari Johnson, Fred Berry, Shirley
Hemphill, and Ernest Thomas in "What's Happening Now!"

"What's Happening Now!"

Syndicated. (1985–1988). Production Company: Columbia Pictures
Television, LBS Communications. Executive Producers: Michael Baser, Kim
Weiskopf. Producers: Mike Milligan, Jay Moriarty, Larry Balmagia, Bob
Peete. Music: Henry Mancini.

Cast. Roger Thomas: Ernest Thomas. Nadine Thomas: Anne-Marie
Johnson: Freddy "Rerun" Stubbs: Fred Berry. Dwayne Clemens: Haywood
Nelson. Shirley Wilson: Shirley Hemphill. Dee Thomas: Danielle Spencer.
Carolyn: Reina King. Maurice Warfield: Martin Lawrence. Darryl: Ken Sagoes.

The Wild Wild West
CBS (9/17/65–9/19/69)

James T. West (Robert Conrad) and Artemus Gordon (Ross Martim) were
secret agents ahead of their time, fighting crime in the Old West from a

gadget-laden train caboose. Time catches up with them ten years later. James West is now an out-of-shape, womanizing saloon owner just south of the border and Artemus Gordon is a traveling Shakespearean actor of little renown. They are unlikely candidates to save the world, but when the son of their old foe Miguelito Loveless (Paul Williams) develops a nuclear bomb, they are the ones the president of the United States reluctantly drafts back into service. However, a lot has changed since West and Gordon were the hottest spies on horseback—their gadgets aren't so amazing, the punches they throw aren't so powerful, and they get out of breath a lot easier. Still, West and Gordon are not to be underestimated, and they rise to the occasion, giving up retirement and getting back into frontier espionage once again.

Background

The two TV revivals were more broadly comic than the original series and, while they did well in the ratings, failed to lead to either a new weekly series or a series of TV movies.

In January 1992, *Variety* reported that Warner Bros, was planning to produce a theatrical version of "The Wild Wild West," directed by Richard Donner, written by Shane Black, and starring Mel Gibson as James West. Two months later, Mel Gibson announced his intention to star in a movie version of Warner Bros,' "Maverick" adaptation as well, also directed by Donner. The Gibson version of "Wild Wild West" never happened. Seven years later, director Barry Sonnenfeld did a "Men in Black" take on the series with Will Smith as James T. West, Kevin Kline as Artemus Gordon, and Kenneth Branagh as Dr. Lovelace. It was a bloated mess that did well at the boxoffice but disappointed critics and fans of the original series.

"The Wild Wild West Revisited"

CBS TV movie (5/9/79). Production Company: CBS Entertainment. Director: Burt Kennedy. Executive Producer: Jay Bernstein. Producer: Robert L. Jacks. Writer: William Bowers. Creator: Michael Garrison. Music: Richard Markowitz.

Cast. James T. West: Robert Conrad. Artemus Gordon: Ross Martin. Miquelito Loveless, Jr.: Paul Williams. Robert T. Malone: Harry Morgan. Capt. Sir David Edney: Rene Auberjonois. Carmelita Loveless: Jo Anne Harris. President Grover Cleveland: Wilford Brimley. Penelope: Trish Noble. Hugo Kaufman: Jeff MacKay.

"More Wild Wild West"

CBS TV movie (10/7/80). Production Company: **cbs** Entertainment. Director: Burt Kennedy. Executive Producer: Jay Bernstein. Producer: Robert L. Jacks. Writers: William Bowers, Tony Kayden.

Cast. James T. West: Robert Conrad. Artemus Gordon: Ross Martin. Prof. Paradine: Jonathan Winters. Robert T. Malone: Harry Morgan. Capt. Sir David Edney: Rene Auberjonois. Dr. Messenger: Victor Buono. Mirabelle: Emma Samms. Juanita: Liz Torres. Jack LaStrange: Jack LaLanne.

WKRP in Cincinnati
CBS (9/17/78–9/20/82)

Radio station WKRP is in big trouble. Seems a D.J. said some naughty words on the air, and now the FCC wants to close the station down, which doesn't particularly bother the wealthy owner, Mrs. Carlson (Carol Bruce), who has wanted to get rid of the money-loser run by her bumbling son Arthur (Gordon Jump) for years. This catastrophe never would have happened if Andy Travis (Gary Sandy) and Baily Quarters (Jan Smithers) were still around to keep Mr. Carlson from hiring the wrong people. But they are gone, as are D.J. Johnny Fever (Howard Hesseman), Mr. Carlson's sexy, brilliant assistant Jennifer Marlowe (Loni Anderson), and D.J. Venus Flytrap (Tim Reid), who is now an executive at Black Entertainment Television. Sleazy sales manager Herb Tarlek (Frank Bonner) and inept newsman Les Nessman (Richard Sanders) are still around—and that's probably half the problem.

But help is on the way. Johnny Fever and Jennifer show up to help save the station, with an able assist from the new program director, Donovan (Mykel

T. Williamson). Once the station is saved, WKRP is back on the airwaves with some new talent—seductive D.J. Mona Loveland (Tawny Kitaen), and a bickering husband and wife team (Michael Des Barres, Kathleen Garrett) doing the morning drive show. Behind the scenes, Herb has competition from an even sleazier salesman—Mr. Carlson's son Arthur Carlson, Jr. (Lightfield Lewis).

Background

"WKRP in Cincinnati" never broke through in a big way on CBS but the reruns did surprisingly well in syndication, prompting stations to back a first-run syndicated revival. The new series, however, only performed modestly, but not good enough to make financial sense for the stations to bankroll it beyond two seasons. One of the studio's primary motivations for reviving the series was to have new episodes to add to the 90 pre-existing reruns in the syndication package. But for unknown reasons, that didn't happen…so the "The New WKRP in Cincinnati" is largely forgotten, except by those who saw it in its original run.

"The New WKRP in Cincinnati"

Syndicated. 30 minutes. 47 episodes. (9/14/91-5/1/93). Production Company: MTM Enterprises. Executive Producer: Bill Dial. Producers: Max Tash, Matt Dinsmore, Ginger Grigg. Story Editors: Gail Honigsberg, Stephen Nathan, Bob Wilcox. Creator: Hugh Wilson.

Cast. Arthur Carlson: Gordon Jump. Herb Tarlek: Frank Bonner. Les Nessman: Richard Sanders. Donovan Aberhold: Mykel T. Williamson. Mona Loveland: Tawny Kitaen. Mrs. Carlson: Carol Bruce. Jack Allen: Michael Des Barres. Dana Burns: Kathleen Garrett. Lucille Tarlek: Edie McClurg. Claire Hartline: Hope Alexander-Willis. Arthur Carlson, Jr.: Lightfield Lewis. Razor D: French Stewart

APPENDIX: ANIMATED REVIVALS

"Addams Family"

NBC. 37 episodes (9/8/73–8/30/75). Producers: William Hanna, Joseph Barbera.

A spinoff from the popular cartoon "Scooby Doo" featuring the further adventures of the altogether ooky Addams Family as they travel cross-country. The animated characters were patterned closely after the Charles Addams *New Yorker* cartoons, rather than the live-action television series. Although John Astin and Carolyn Jones returned for the "Scooby Doo" guest spot, only Jackie Coogan and Ted Cassidy reprised their roles in the animated series, while Lennie Weinrib (Gomez), Janet Waldo (Morticia and Grandmama), Cindy Henderson (Wednesday), and Jodie Foster (Pugsley) provided the other voices.

"The New Adventures of Gilligan"

ABC (9/7/74–9/4/77). Producers: Norm Prescott, Lou Scheimer.

More of the same, only animated, with all the cast members returning for voices, with the exception of Ginger and Mary Ann, who were assayed by Jane Webb and Jane Edwards.

"Gilligan's Planet"

CBS (9/18/82–9/10/83). Producers: Norm Prescott, Lou Scheimer.

When the castaways attempt to escape the island on a rocket, they end up crash landing on an uncharted planet instead. Again, the cast returned, with Dawn Wells doing double duty as both Ginger and Mary Ann.

"Jeannie"

CBS (9/8/73–8/30/75). Producers: William Hanna, Joseph Barbera.

Loosely based on the television series. In this version, a teenage boy (Mark Hamill) finds a bottle and rubs it, and out pops Jeannie (Julie McWhirter), a beautiful teenage genie.

"Lost in Space"

ABC 60 minutes (9/8/73) Production Company: 20th Century Fox Television, Hanna-Barbera Productions. Producers: Joseph Barbera, William Hanna.

Aired as an episode of "ABC Saturday Superstar Movie," aka "The New Saturday Superstar Movie," an anthology that was a platform for burning off pilots for proposed animated series based on old TV series, movies and books.

In this "reimagining" of "Lost in Space," Biology professor Dr. Smith (Jonathan Harris), a geologist (Dodi Carmichael) and young Linc Robinson (Timothy Van Patten) are the passengers of an interplanetary space shuttle piloted by Craig Robinson (Michael Bell) and a robot named "Robon." The ship encounters a meteor storm that hurls them into an uncharted corner of the universe. Other voice actors included Don Messick, Sidney Miller, and Ralph James.

"Nanny and the Professor"

ABC 60 minutes. (9/30/72) Production Company: Fred Calvert Productions, Universal Television. Producer: Fred Calvert. Writers: Arthur Alsberg, Don Nelson.

Aired as an episode of "ABC Saturday Superstar Movie." The original sitcom, a riff on "The Sound of Music" (only without the music), starred Richard Long as a widowed professor who hires eccentric British nanny Phoebe Figalily, played by Juliet Mills, to help him raise his three kids (Kim Richards, David Doremus, Trent Lehman). In this story, which featured all of the original cast returning to voice their characters, the family, Phoebe, and her Aunt Henrietta (Joan Gerber) recover a stolen microdot and have to evade bad guys to return it to the authorities.

"Nanny and the Professor and the Phantom of the Circus"

ABC 60 minutes (11/17/73) Production Company, Fred Calvert Productions, Universal Television. Producer: Fred Calvert. Writers: Arthur Alsberg, Don Nelson.

The family, Phoebe, and zany Aunt Henrietta solve a "Scooby-Doo"-esque mystery at her traveling circus. Voice cast included Walter Edmiston, Paul Shively and Dave Ketchum.

"My Favorite Martians"

CBS (9/8/73–8/30/75). Producers: Norm Prescott, Lou Scheimer.

Loosely based on the television series. This time, Uncle Martin (Jonathan Harris) crash lands on Earth with his nephew Andy (Edward Morris) and their space dog. The three aliens move in with reporter Tim O'Hara (Lane Scheimer) and his niece Kay (Jane Webb).

"The Munsters"

ABC 60 minutes. (10/27/73) Production Company: Fred Calvert Productions, Universal Television. Director: Gerald Baldwin. Writers: Arthur Alsberg, Don Nelson.

Aired as an episode of "ABC Saturday Superstar Movie." The Munsters return in this story about Eddie Munster forming a band with his cousins, Igor and Lucretia, who drive a hearse that's powered by music. Al Lewis was the only member of the original cast who returned while Richard Long (Herman Munster), Cynthia Adler (Lily Munster), and Stuart Getz (Eddie

Munster) stepped in for the rest of the family. Other voice actors included Arnold Stang, Henry Gibson, Bobby Diamond, Paul Shively, Ron Feinberg.

"Star Trek"

NBC. 22 episodes (9/8/73–8/30/75). Producers: Norm Prescott, Lou Scheimer. Director: Hal Sutherland. Story Editor: D.C. Fontana.

The further adventures of the starship *Enterprise* in this highly acclaimed animated continuation, which won an Emmy Award for outstanding children's programming. The cast returned to provide their voices, with James Doohan doing double duty as both Scott and a new alien helmsman. Also returning were several writers of the original series, some of whom penned sequels to their live-action episodes. Sequel episodes were "More Tribbles, More Troubles," "Mudd's Passion," "Yesteryear" and "Once Upon a Planet."

"That Girl in Wonderland"

ABC 60 minutes. (1/13/73) Production Company: Rankin-Bass. Directors: Jules Bass, Arthur Rankin. Producer: Basil Cox. Writers: Stu Hample.

Aired as an episode of "ABC Saturday Superstar Movie." A bizarre adaptation of the hit situation comedy that starred Marlo Thomas as Ann-Marie, an aspiring actress romantically involved with magazine reporter in New York City. Now, she imagines herself as the heroine in classic stories like "Alice in Wonderland" and "Cinderella." Thomas returned to voice the character. Other voice actors included Patricia Bright, Ted Schwartz, Dick Heymeyer, Rhoda Mann.

APPENDIX: TELEVISION SERIES REVIVALS
1992-2015

Here's a list of television series revivals – those TV shows and feature films that featured *some or all of the original cast members reprising their roles*—that were produced since the first edition of this book published (and following the same inclusion criteria). Only the titles, formats, and airdates are included here. You'll have to wait until the next volume of this book for more detailed entries on the shows…

ALF
   Project Alf (2/14/96) ABC TV Movie
ALIEN NATION
   Dark Horizon (10/25/94) Fox TV Movie
   Body and Soul (10/10/95) Fox TV Movie
   Millenium (1/2/96) Fox TV Movie
   Enemy Within (11/12/96) Fox TV Movie
   Udara Legacy (7/29/97) Fox TV Movie
ARRESTED DEVELOPMENT
   Arrested Development (premiered 5/26/13) Netflix series
BEVERLY HILLBILLIES
   Legend of the Beverly Hillbillies (5/24/93) CBS Special
BEVERLY HILLS 90210
   Beverly Hills 90210 (9/2/08-5/13/13) CW series
BIONIC WOMAN
   Bionic Ever After (11/29/94) CBS TV Movie
BOY MEETS WORLD
   Girl Meets World (1/27/2014-present) Disney series
BURKE'S LAW
   Burke's Law (1/7/94-7/27/95) CBS series

CAGNEY & LACEY

The Return (11/6/94) CBS TV Movie

Together Again (5/2/95) CBS TV Movie

View Through the Glass Ceiling (10/25/95) CBS TV Movie

True Convictions (1/29/96) CBS TV Movie

CHIPS

CHIPS '99 (10/27/98) TBS TV Movie

CHRISTY

Christy The Movie (11/19/00) PAX TV Movie

Choices of the Heart (5/13 & 14/01) PAX TV Movie

COACH

Coach (2015) NBC Series

DALLAS

Dallas: JR Returns (11/15/96) CBS TV Movie

Dallas: War of the Ewings (4/24/98) CBS TV Movie

Dallas (6/13/12-9/22/14) TNT series

DICK VAN DYKE SHOW

Dick Van Dyke Show Revisited (5/9/04) CBS special

DUKES OF HAZZARD

The Reunion (4/25/97) CBS TV Movie

Dukes of Hazzard in Hollywood (5/19/00) CBS TV Movie

ENTOURAGE

Entourage (2015) Feature Film

FARSCAPE

The Peacekeeper Wars (10/17/04) Syfy TV Movie

FACTS OF LIFE

Facts of Life Reunion (11/18/01) ABC TV Movie

FIREFLY

Serenity (2005) Feature Film

FULL HOUSE

Full House (2015) Netflix series

GET SMART

Get Smart Again (2/26/89) ABC TV Movie

Get Smart (1/14/95-2/19/95) Fox series

GREATEST AMERICAN HERO

Greatest American Heroine Unaired 1997 NBC pilot

GROWING PAINS
Growing Pains: The Movie (11/5/00) ABC TV Movie
Return of the Seavers (10/16/04) ABC TV Movie

GUNSMOKE
The Long Ride (5/8/93) CBS TV Movie
One Man's Justice (2/10/94) CBS TV Movie

HART TO HART
Hart to Hart Returns (11/5/93) NBC TV Movie
Home is Where the Hart Is (2/18/94) NBC TV Movie
Crimes of the Hart (3/25/94) NBC TV Movie
Old Friends Never Die (5/6/94) NBC TV Movie
Secrets of the Hart (3/6/95) NBC TV Movie
Two Harts in 3/4 Time (11/26/95) Family Channel TV Movie
Harts in High Season (3/24/96) Family Channel TV Movie
Til Death Do Us Hart (8/25/96) Family Channel TV Movie

HAWAII FIVE-O
Hawaii Five-O (Unaired 1997) CBS pilot

HEROES
Heroes Reborn (2015) NBC series

HUNTER
Everyone Walks in LA (6/6/95) NBC TV Movie
Return to Justice (11/16/02) NBC TV Movie
Back in Force (4/12/03) NBC TV Movie
Hunter (4/19/2003-5/3/2003) NBC series

IRONSIDE
Return of Ironside (5/4/93) NBC TV movie

I SPY
I Spy Returns (2/3/94) CBS TV movie

KNIGHTRIDER
Knightrider (2/17/2008) NBC TV Movie

KOJAK
Fatal Flaw (11/30/89) ABC TV Movie
Ariana (4/7/90) ABC TV Movie
Flowers for Matty (1/4/90) ABC TV Movie
It's Always Something (2/3/90) ABC TV Movie
None so Blind (4/7/90) ABC TV Movie

KUNG FU

Kung Fu: The Legend Continues (1/27/93-1/1/97) Syndicated Series

KNOTS LANDING

Back to the Cul-de-Sac (5/7/97) CBS Miniseries

LA LAW

LA Law: The Movie (5/12/02) NBC TV Movie

LOVE BOAT

The Next Wave (4/13/98-5/21/99) UPN series

MacGYVER

Lost Treasure of Atlantis (5/14/94) ABC TV Movie

Trail to Doomsday (11/24/94) ABC TV Movie

MANNIX

Hard-Boiled Murder (2/13/97) CBS (*Diagnosis Murder* Episode)

MARY TYLER MOORE

Mary & Rhoda (2/7/00) ABC TV Movie

MATLOCK

Murder One (1/30/97) & (2/6/97) CBS (*Diagnosis Murder* episode)

MELROSE PLACE

Melrose Place (9/8/2009-4/13/2010) CW series

MIKE HAMMER

Mike Hammer, Private Eye (9/27/97-6/14/98) Syndicated Series

MISSION IMPOSSIBLE

Discards (11/13/97) CBS (*Diagnosis Murder* episode)

MURDER SHE WROTE

South By Southwest (11/2/97) CBS TV Movie

A Story To Die For (5/18/00) CBS TV Movie

The Last Free Man (5/2/01) CBS TV Movie

The Celtic Riddle (5/9/03) CBS TV Movie

THE ODD COUPLE

The Odd Couple: Together Again (9/24/93) CBS TV Movie

POLICE SQUAD

The Naked Gun: From the Files of Police Squad! (1988) Feature Film

The Naked Gun 2½: The Smell of Fear (1991) Feature Film

The Naked Gun 33⅓: The Final Insult (1994) Feature Film

PRETENDER

The Pretender 2001 (1/22/01) TNT TV Movie

Island of the Haunted (12/10/01) TNT TV Movie

ROCKFORD FILES

I Still Love LA (11/27/94) CBS TV Movie

A Blessing in Disguise (5/14/95) CBS TV Movie

If the Frame Fits (1/14/96) CBS TV Movie

Godfather Knows Best (2/18/96) CBS TV Movie

Friends and Foul Play (4/25/96) CBS TV Movie

Punishment and Crime (9/18/96) CBS TV Movie

Murders and Misdemeanors (11/21/97) CBS TV Movie

If It Bleeds, It Leads (4/20/99) CBS TV Movie

SEX AND THE CITY

Sex and the City: The Movie (2008) Feature Film

Sex and the City 2 (2010) Feature Film

SIMON AND SIMON

In Trouble Again (2/23/95) CBS TV Movie

SIX MILLION DOLLAR MAN

Bionic Ever After (11/29/94) CBS TV Movie

SPENSER FOR HIRE

Ceremony (7/22/93) Lifetime TV Movie

Pale Kings and Horses (1/2/94) Lifetime TV Movie

The Judas Goat (12/1/94) Lifetime TV Movie

A Savage Place (1995) Lifetime TV Movie

THE COMEBACK

The Comeback (premiered 11/09/14) HBO series

THE DEFENDERS

Payback (10/12/1997) Showtime TV Movie

Choice of Evils (1/15/98) Showtime TV Movie

Taking the First (10/25/98) Showtime TV Movie

THE INVADERS

The Invaders (11/12/95-11/14/95) Fox Miniseries

THE MONKEES

Hey Hey It's the Monkees (2/17/97) ABC TV Movie

24

Live Another Day (premiered 5/5/14) Fox Miniseries

TWIN PEAKS

Twin Peaks: Fire Walk with Me Feature Film

VERONICA MARS

Veronica Mars (2014) Feature Film

WALTONS

A Walton Thanksgiving Reunion (11/21/93) CBS TV Movie

A Wedding Reunion (2/12/95) CBS TV Movie

A Walton Easter (3/30/97) CBS TV Movie

WALKER TEXAS RANGER

Trial By Fire (10/16/05) CBS TV Movie

WISEGUY

Return of Vinnie Terranova (5/2/96) ABC TV Movie

X-FILES

X-Files For the Future (1998) Feature Film

X Files: I Want to Believe (2008) Feature Film

X-Files (2015) Fox Series

APPENDIX: TELEVISION SERIES REMAKES 1992-2015

Here's a list of TV shows that were remade/rebooted with new actors and, in some cases, very different formats, on television and in the movies since the original publication of this book (and following the same inclusion criteria)

A-TEAM
A-Team (2010) Feature Film
ALL IN THE FAMILY
704 Hauser Street (4/11/94-5/9/94) CBS TV Series
THE AVENGERS
The Avengers (1998) Feature Film
BATTLESTAR GALACTICA
Battlestar Galactica (10/18/2004-3/20/2009) SyFy Network Series
BEAUTY AND THE BEAST
Beauty and the Beast (premiere 10/11/12) CW TV Series
THE BEVERLY HILLBILLIES
Beverly Hillbillies (1993) Feature Film
BEWITCHED
Bewitched (2005) Feature Film
BIONIC WOMAN
The Bionic Woman (9/26/07-11/28/07) NBC Series
BONANZA
The Return (11/28/93) NBC TV Movie
Under Attack (1/15/95) NBC TV Movie
Ponderosa (9/9/01-5/12/02) PAX TV Series
BRADY BUNCH
The Brady Bunch Movie (1995) Feature Film
A Very Brady Sequel (1996) Feature Film

Brady Bunch in the White House (2002) Fox TV Movie

CAR 54, WHERE ARE YOU?

Car 54, Where Are You (1994) Feature Film

CHARLIE'S ANGELS

Charlie's Angels (2000) Feature Film

Charlie's Angels Full Throttle (2003) Feature Film

Charlie's Angels (9/22/11-11/10/11) ABC TV Series

CUPID

Cupid (3/31/09-6/16/09) ABC TV Series

DRAGNET

Dragnet / LA Dragnet (5/11/03-5/5/04) ABC series

DUKES OF HAZZARD

Dukes of Hazzard (2005) Feature Film

Dukes of Hazzard: The Beginning (2007) TV Movie

ELECTRA WOMAN & DYNA GIRL

Electra Woman & Dyna Girl (2001) CW Pilot

THE EQUALIZER

The Equalizer (2015) Feature Film

FAMILY AFFAIR

Family Affair (9/2/2002-3/13/2003) CW Series

FANTASY ISLAND

Fantasy Island (9/26/98-1/24/99) ABC Series

FLIPPER

Flipper: The New Adventures (10/2/95-7/1/2000) Syndicated Series

Flipper (1996) Feature Film

THE FLINTSTONES

The Flintstones (1994) Feature Film

The Flintstones: Viva Rock Vegas (2000) Feature Film

THE FUGITIVE

The Fugitive (1993) Feature Film

The Fugitive (10/6/00-5/25/01) CBS TV Series

GET SMART

Get Smart (2008) Feature Film

HAWAII FIVE-O

Hawaii Five-O (premiered 9/20/10) CBS Series

THE HONEYMOONERS

The Honeymooners (2005) Feature Film

IRONSIDE

Ironside (10/2/13-10/23/13) NBC TV Series

I SPY

I Spy (2002) Feature Film

KNIGHTRIDER

Knightrider 2010 (2/13/94) Syndicated TV Movie

Team Knightrider (10/6/97-5/18/98) Syndicated series

Knightrider (9/24/08-3/4/09) NBC TV Series

KOJAK

Kojak (3/25/05-5/22/05) USA Network Series

LAND OF THE LOST

Land of the Lost (9/7/91-12/5/92) ABC TV Series

Land of the Lost (2009) Feature Film

LOST IN SPACE

Lost In Space (1998) Feature Film

The Robinsons (2004) Unaired CW Pilot

THE MAN FROM UNCLE

The Man From Uncle (2015) Feature Film

MAVERICK

Maverick (1994) Feature Film

McHALE'S NAVY

McHale's Navy (1997) Feature Film

MIAMI VICE

Miami Vice (2006) Feature Film

MISSION IMPOSSIBLE

Mission Impossible (1996) Feature Film

Mission Impossible 2 (2000) Feature Film

Mission Impossible 3 (2006) Feature Film

Mission Impossible Ghost Protocol (2011) Feature Film

Mission Impossible: Rogue Nation (2015) Feature Film

THE MUNSTERS

Mockingbird Lane (10/26/12) NBC Pilot

MY FAVORITE MARTIAN

My Favorite Martian (1999) Feature Film

THE NIGHT STALKER

The Night Stalker (9/29/05-2/7/06) ABC Series

THE PRISONER

The Prisoner (11/15/09-11/17/09) AMC Miniseries

ROCKFORD FILES

The Rockford Files (2010) Unaired NBC Pilot

ROUTE 66

Route 66 (6/8/93-7/6/93) NBC Series

SGT. BILKO

Sgt. Bilko (1996) Feature Film

STAR TREK

Star Trek (2009) Feature Film

Star Trek Into Darkness (2013) Feature Film

STARSKY AND HUTCH

Starsky & Hutch (2004) Feature Film

S.W.A.T

S.W.A.T (2003) Feature Film

TIME TUNNEL

Time Tunnel (2006) Unaired Pilot Fox

21 JUMP STREET

21 Jump Street (2012) Feature Film

22 Jump Street (2014) Feature Film

V

V (11/3/09-3/15/11) ABC TV Series

WILD WILD WEST

Wild Wild West (1999) Feature Film

BIBLIOGRAPHY

Bedell, Sally. *Up the Tube: Primetime TV and the Silverman Years*. New York: Viking, 1981.

Brooks, Tim, and Earl Marsh. *The Complete Directory of Primetime Network TV Shows 1946-Present*, revised edition. New York: Ballantine, 1981.

Christensen, Mark, and Cameron Stauth. *The Sweeps: Behind the Scenes in Network TV*. New York: William Morrow, 1984.

Cox, Stephen. *The Addams Family Chronicles*. New York: HarperCollins, 1991.

_____. *The Munsters: TV's First Family of Fright*. New York: Contemporary Books, 1989.

Edelstein, Andrew J., and Frank Lovece. *The Brady Bunch Book*. New York: Warner, 1991.

Eisner, Joel, and David Krinsky. *Television Comedy Series: An Episode Guide to 153 TV Sitcoms in Syndication*. Jefferson, N.C.: McFarland, 1984.

Fireman, Judy. *TV Book*. New York: Workman, 1977.

Gerani, Gary, and Paul S. Schulman. *Fantastic Television*. New York: Harmony Books, 1977.

Gianakos, Larry James. *Television Drama Series Programming: A Comprehensive Chronicle, 1959–1975*. Metuchen, N.J.: Scarecrow, 1978.

_____. *Television Drama Series Programming: 1947–1959*. Metuchen, N.J.: Scarecrow, 1980.

_____. *Television Drama Series Programming: 1975–1980*. Metuchen, N.J.: Scarecrow, 1981.

_____. *Television Drama Series Programming: 1980–1982*. Metuchen, N.J.: Scarecrow, 1983.

Gitlin, Todd. *Inside Primetime*. New York: Pantheon, 1983.

Goldberg, Lee. *Unsold Television Pilots 1955–1988*. Jefferson, N.C.: McFarland, 1990.

_____. *Unsold TV Pilots*, abridged/updated edition. New York: Citadel, 1991.

Grossman, Gary. *Saturday Morning Cartoons*. New York: Arlington House, 1987.

Heitland, Jon. *The Man from UNCLE Book*. New York: St. Martin's Press, 1988.

Kelly, Richard. *The Andy Griffith Show*, revised and expanded edition. Winston-Salem, N.C.: John F. Blair, 1984.

McCarty, John, and Brian Kelleher. *Alfred Hitchcock Presents*. New York: St. Martin's Press, 1985. McCrohan, Donna. *The Life & Times of Maxwell Smart*. New York: St. Martin's Press, 1988.

McNeil, Alex. *Total Television: A Comprehensive Guide to Programming from 1948 to the Present*, third edition. New York: Penguin, 1991.

Maltin, Leonard. *TV Movies and Video Guide*, 1992 edition. New York: New American Library, 1991.

Marill, Alvin H. *Movies Made for Television: The Telefeature and the Mini-Series*. New York: New York Zoetrope, 1987.

Meyers, Richard. *TV Detectives*. San Diego, CA: A.S. Barnes, 1981.

Mitz, Rick. *The Great TV Sitcom Book*, expanded edition. New York: Perigee Books, 1983.

Perry, Jeb H. *Universal Television: The Studio and Its Programs, 1950–1980*. Metuchen, N.J.: Scarecrow, 1983. Rogers, Dave. *The Avengers*. London: Independent Television Books, 1983.

Scheuer, Steven H. *Movies on TV*. New York: Bantam, 1982.

_____. *The Television Annual 1978–79*. New York: Collier, 1979.

Schwartz, Sherwood. *Inside Gilligan's Island: From Creation to Syndication*. Jefferson, N.C.: McFarland, 1988.

Terrace, Vincent. *Encyclopedia of Television: Series, Pilots and Specials 1974–1984*. New York: New York Zoetrope, 1985.

_____. *Encyclopedia of Television: Series, Pilots and Specials 1936–1973*. New York: New York Zoetrope, 1986.

_____. *Encyclopedia of Television: Series, Pilots and Specials. The Index: Who's Who in Television 1937–1984*. New York: New York Zoetrope, 1986.

_____. *Fifty Years of Television: A Guide to Series & Pilots, 1937–1988*. New York: Cornwall Books, 1991.

_____. *Ultimate TV Trivia*. Boston: Faber and Faber, 1991.

White, Patrick J. *The Complete Mission Impossible Dossier.* New York: Avon, 1991.

Woolley, Lynn, Robert W. Malsbary, and Robert G. Strange, Jr. *Warner Brothers Television.* Jefferson, N.C.: McFarland, 1985.

Zicree, Marc Scott. *The Twilight Zone Companion.* New York: Bantam, 1982.

ABOUT THE AUTHOR

Lee Goldberg is a two-time Edgar Award and Shamus Award nominee whose many TV writing and/or producing credits include *Martial Law, SeaQuest, Diagnosis Murder, The Cosby Mysteries, Hunter, Spenser: For Hire, Nero Wolfe, The Glades* and *Monk*. His many books include *The Walk, King City, Successful Television Writing, Watch Me Die*, the *Diagnosis Murder* and *Monk* series of original mystery novels, and the internationally bestselling Fox & O'Hare series that he co-authors with Janet Evanovich. As a TV development consultant, he's worked for production companies and broadcasters in Germany, Spain, Sweden, and the Netherlands.

INDEX